You've got this.

This is the final stretch of your CPA Exam preparation – the Final Review. You've diligently studied these topics, and now it's crunch time. This Final Review has completely new content from the Becker CPA Exam Review and focuses on the key concepts on the CPA Exam. Remember, fortune favors the brave, but the CPA Exam favors the prepared.

Access Becker's Final Review

You can access Final Review under Additional Resources on each section home page when you log in to **cpa.becker.com** or when you use the mobile apps.

What's inside

Your Final Review is designed to mimic the actual CPA Exam, and has all-new task-based simulations with SkillMaster videos and all-new multiple-choice questions. If you need help at any point, remember that you still have access to the features of the CPA Exam Review, including:

- SkillMaster videos that coach you through task-based simulations in the four-part CPA course

- Access to 1-on-1 academic support from our experienced CPA instructors

- Unlimited practice tests to work on your weaknesses

You're not in it alone!

For tips, stories and advice, visit our blog at **becker.com/blog.** You can also collaborate with other Becker students studying BEC on our Facebook study group at **facebook.com/groups/ BeckerBECStudyGroup/.**

Exam day tips

We want you to be prepared and confident when exam day rolls around. Here are some tips to keep in mind:

+ Arrive at least 30 minutes early on exam day.

+ Bring your NTS and two forms of identification.

+ Your cell phone is NOT allowed in the testing center, even during scheduled breaks.

+ No outside calculators are allowed. The testing software will have a built-in calculator for you to use.

+ Breathe. Relax. Ground yourself. You've got this.

Join the community!

Becker™

This textbook contains information that was current at the time of printing.
Your course software will be updated on a regular basis as the content
that is tested on the CPA Exam evolves and as we improve our materials.
Note the version reference below and select your replacement textbook
under Replacement Products at **becker.com/cpa-replacement-products**
to learn if a newer version of this book is available to be ordered.

CPA Exam Review

Business
Final Review

For Exams Scheduled
After June 30, 2021

V 4.0

COURSE DEVELOPMENT TEAM

Timothy F. Gearty, CPA, MBA, JD, CGMA . . . . Editor in Chief, Financial/Regulation (Tax) National Editor

Angeline S. Brown, CPA, CGMA. . . . . Sr. Director, Product Management

Michael Potenza, CPA, JD. . . . . Director, Curriculum

Stephen Bergens, CPA. . . . . Manager, Accounting Curriculum

Cheryl Costello, CPA, CGMA . . . . Sr. Specialist, Curriculum

Tom Cox, CPA, CMA . . . . Financial (GASB & NFP) National Editor

Steven J. Levin, JD . . . . Regulation (Law) National Editor

Danita De Jane . . . . Director, Course Development

Joe Antonio . . . . Manager, Course Development

Shelly McCubbins, MBA. . . . . Project Manager, Course Development

CONTRIBUTING EDITORS

Teresa C. Anderson, CPA, CMA, MPA

Valerie Funk Anderson, CPA

Heather Baiye, CPA, MBA

Katie Barnette, CPA

Elliott G. Chester, CPA, CMA, CFE

Courtney Chianello, CPA

Jim DeSimpelare, CPA, MBA

Tara Z. Fisher, CPA

Melisa F. Galasso, CPA

R. Thomas Godwin, CPA, CGMA

Holly Hawk, CPA, CGMA

Liliana Hickman-Riggs, CPA, CMA, CIA, CFE, CITP, CFF, CGMA, FCPA, MS

Patrice W. Johnson, CPA

Julie D. McGinty, CPA

Sandra McGuire, CPA, MBA

Stephanie Morris, CPA, MAcc

Michelle Moshe, CPA, DipIFR

Peter Olinto, JD, CPA

Sandra Owen, JD, MBA, CPA

Michelle M. Pace, CPA

Jennifer J. Rivers, CPA

Josh Rosenberg, MBA, CPA, CFA, CFP

Jonathan R. Rubin, CPA, MBA

Michael Rybak, CPA, CFA

Jacob Shortt, CPA

Denise M. Stefano, CPA, CGMA, MBA

Elizabeth Lester Walsh, CPA, CITP

Permissions

Material from *Uniform CPA Examination Selected Questions and Unofficial Answers*, 1989–2021, copyright © by American Institute of Certified Public Accountants, Inc., is reprinted and/or adapted with permission.

Any knowing solicitation or disclosure of any questions or answers included on any CPA Examination is prohibited.

Business

Final Review Sections

Business Section I | *Corporate Governance*

A   Corporate Governance

Business Section II | *Economic Concepts and Analysis*

A   Economic and Business Cycles

B   Market Influences on Business

C   Financial Risk Management

Business Section III | *Financial Management*

A   Capital Structure

B   Working Capital

C   Financial Valuation Methods

D   Financial Decision Models

Business Section IV | *Information Technology*

A   Information Technology (IT) Governance

B   The Role of IT in Business

C   Data Management and Analytics

D   System Development and Change Management

E   IT Risks and Responses

Business Section V | *Operations Management*

A   Performance Management

B   Cost Accounting

C   Process Management

D   Budgeting and Analysis

E   Forecasting and Projection

Introduction

Final Review is a condensed review that reinforces your understanding of the most heavily tested concepts on the CPA Exam. It is designed to help focus your study time during those final days between your Becker CPA Exam Review course and your exam date.

This Book

Becker's Final Review is arranged based on the AICPA's blueprints. The blueprints outline the technical content to be tested on each of the four parts of the CPA Exam. The blueprints can be found in the back sections of Becker's main CPA textbooks.

The Software

The Final Review software uses an interactive eBook (IEB) format. Watch the introduction video in the Final Review software for a tour of the IEB features.

We recommend progressing through this course in the following order:

- Review the IEB content, including the video introduction to each topic and the lecture audio associated with each page of the IEB.
- Work the embedded multiple-choice questions for each topic as you progress through the content.
- Work the related multiple-choice questions in the question bank for each topic.
- Once you have completed all of the IEB sections, topics, and multiple-choice questions, do the practice Simulations in the software.

Becker Customer and Academic Support

You can access Becker's Customer and Academic Support from within the course software by clicking Contact Support at the top at:

cpa.becker.com

You can also access customer service and technical support by calling 1-877-CPA-EXAM (outside the U.S. +1-630-472-2213).

I | Corporate Governance

A Corporate Governance

1 Rights, Duties, Responsibilities, and Authority of the Board of Directors and Officers

1.1 Board of Directors

Among the specific duties of directors are the election, removal, and supervision of officers; adoption, amendment, and repeal of bylaws; setting management compensation; initiating fundamental changes to the corporation's structure; and declaration of distributions to owners. Another critical role of the board is to manage any potential conflict of interest that may exist between the shareholders (principal) and senior management (agent). Directors are fiduciaries of the corporation and must always act in the best interests of the corporation.

1.2 Officers

Officers are corporate agents. Officers are fiduciaries of the corporation and must act in the best interests of the corporation. Officers may serve on the board of directors and are not required to be shareholders.

2 Sarbanes-Oxley Act of 2002

The financial reporting issues associated with corporate governance generally relate to the provisions of the Sarbanes-Oxley Act of 2002 (also known as SOX). SOX has numerous provisions for expanded disclosures and specific representations by management that are described in the first two major titles.

2.1 Title III—Corporate Responsibility

- Public companies (also known as issuers) must have an audit committee.

- The audit committee comprises board members who are independent of the company other than their membership on the board of directors. To be independent, an audit committee member cannot be a paid consultant or advisor.

- The external auditor reports to the audit committee.

- The chief executive officer (CEO) and the chief financial officer (CFO) are required to sign off on published reports and represent that the report:

  - was reviewed by each party.

  - does not contain untrue statements or material omissions.

  - contains financial statements that present fairly in all material respects the financial condition and results of operations of the issuer.

- The CEO and CFO are required to represent that they are responsible for internal controls and that the controls are designed to ensure that all material information has been made available to the auditors, and that controls have been evaluated for effectiveness.

- The CEO and CFO must represent whether there have been any significant changes to internal control.

- If the CEO or CFO falsify information about the financial statements, potential penalties include repaying the issuer any bonuses that are equity based or repaying any gains that were realized on the sale of the issuer's stock.

2.2 Title IV—Enhanced Financial Disclosures

- Management must include the following enhanced disclosures in its periodic reports.

  - Material correcting adjustments identified by the auditor should be reflected in the financial statements.

  - Disclosure of all material off-balance sheet transactions.

  - Conformity of pro forma financial statements to certain requirements (no untrue statements or omitted material information; reconciled with GAAP financial statements).

  - The use of special purpose entities (SPEs).

- Disclose any parties that have a direct or indirect ownership of more than 10 percent of any class of most equity securities.

- Management must assess the organization's internal controls and make disclosure of that assessment.

- An issuer must disclose whether or not its senior officers have adopted a code of ethics (conduct). If not adopted, the issuer must explain the reasons.

- Audit committees should have a financial expert.

  - The financial expert is an individual who has expertise developed through education or experience as an auditor or finance officer for an organization of similar complexity.

  - The financial expert must be disclosed.

2.3 Title VIII—Corporate and Criminal Fraud Accountability

- An individual who alters, destroys, conceals, or makes false entries in any record or document with the intent to impede, obstruct, or influence an investigation will be fined, imprisoned not more than 20 years, or both.

- Auditors of issuers should retain all audit and review workpapers for a period of seven years from the end of the fiscal period in which the audit or review was conducted. Failure to do so will result in a fine, imprisonment for not more than 10 years, or both.

- The statute of limitations for securities fraud is no later than the earlier of two years after the discovery of the facts constituting the violation or five years after the violation.

- An employee who lawfully provides evidence of fraud may not be discharged, demoted, suspended, threatened, harassed, or in any other manner discriminated against for providing such information.

- An individual who knowingly executes, or attempts to execute, securities fraud will be fined, imprisoned not more than 25 years, or both.

2.4 Title IX—White-Collar Crime Penalty Enhancements

- An individual who attempts or conspires to commit any white-collar offense will be subject to the penalties as predetermined by the United States Sentencing Commission.

- When an issuer files a periodic report with the SEC that contains financial statements, it must include the following written statements (signatures):

  - The report fully complies with the Securities Exchange Act of 1934.

  - The information contained in the report fairly presents, in all material respects, the financial condition and operating results of the issuer.

  - The above written statements must be signed by the chief executive officer and chief financial officer (or their equivalent) of the issuer, who bear full responsibility for these written statements.

- When a party of the issuer certifies a financial report and/or its contents, knowing that it does not satisfy all three requirements above, he or she will be subject to fines or imprisonment.

2.5 Title XI—Corporate Fraud Accountability

- An individual who alters the integrity of, destroys, or conceals a document used in connection with an official proceeding shall be fined and/or subject to not more than a 20-year prison term.

- As part of cease-and-desist proceedings, the SEC may issue an order that prohibits a person from serving as an officer or director of an issuer, in the event the SEC determines that the person has violated securities rules/regulations and is unfit to continue to serve the issuer in that capacity.

- An individual who knowingly retaliates against a person who provides truthful information to the SEC in connection with a possible federal offense shall be fined or imprisoned for not more than 10 years.

Which of the following is true regarding a financial expert serving on the audit committee of an issuer that is complying with the Sarbanes-Oxley Act of 2002?

1. The audit committee member may qualify for recognition as a financial expert using most any combination of education and experience auditing or preparing financial reports.

2. An audit committee member must have been a member of the board of directors for five years before serving as a financial expert.

3. An audit committee member qualifying as a financial expert must have adequate technical training and experience as an auditor.

4. Disclosure of the financial expert is made at the election of the audit committee.

3 Internal Control

The Committee of Sponsoring Organizations (COSO) issued *Internal Control—Integrated Framework* (the Framework) to assist organizations in developing comprehensive assessments of internal control effectiveness. COSO's framework is widely regarded as an appropriate and comprehensive basis to document the assessment of internal controls over financial reporting.

3.1 COSO Framework Objectives

There are three categories of objectives built within the framework:

1. **Operating Objectives:** These pertain to the effectiveness and efficiency of an entity's operations.

2. **Reporting Objectives:** These relate to the reliability, timeliness, and transparency of an entity's external and internal financial and nonfinancial reporting.

3. **Compliance Objectives:** These are developed to ensure the entity is adhering to existing laws and regulations.

3.2 COSO Framework

The COSO framework comprises five integrated components that logically begin with the tone at the top and conclude with monitoring the effectiveness of internal controls. There are 17 principles that support these 5 components. The mnemonic "**CRIME**" is used to remember these 5 components.

3.2.1 Control Environment

- Referred to as the "tone at the top."

- Ethics, board oversight, commitment to employee competencies, and organizational structure are the foundational principles that define this component.

3.2.2 Risk Assessment

- Identification and analysis of risks related to the entity's objectives is performed under the risk assessment component.

- Organizational objectives, risk and fraud identification, and assessing changes that impact internal control are principles of this component.

3.2.3 Information and Communication

- This principle includes capturing and processing information.

- Financial reporting and internal control information as well as internal and external communication are supporting principles of the information and communication component.

3.2.4 Monitoring

- Monitoring the effectiveness of internal control is the goal of the monitoring component.

- Monitoring by way of ongoing and separate evaluations and reporting findings (deficiencies) are the related principles.

3.2.5 (Existing) Control Activities

- The policies and procedures that respond to the risk assessment are the subject of the control activities component.

- Principles of (existing) control activities include selecting and developing control activities, developing technological controls, and deploying policies and procedures.

3.3 COSO Cube

The three-dimensional COSO cube demonstrates that there is a direct relationship between an entity's three framework objectives, its five integrated internal control components, and the organizational structure of the entity.

© 2013 Committee of Sponsoring Organizations of the Treadway Commission (COSO). Used by permission.

3.4 Effective (Ineffective) Internal Control—COSO

- The framework defines an effective internal control system as one that provides reasonable assurance that the entity's objectives will be achieved. The framework general requirements include:

  - Five components and 17 principles that are relevant are to be both present and functioning.

  - All five components operating together as an integrated system are a means to reduce the risk to an acceptable level that the entity will not achieve its objectives.

- In order to be considered an effective system of internal control, senior management and the board must achieve reasonable assurance (meet specific requirements) that the entity:

  - understands when its operations are managed effectively and efficiently.

  - complies with applicable rules, regulations, and external standards.

  - prepares financial reports that conform to the entity's reporting objectives and all applicable rules, regulations, and standards.

- When a major deficiency is identified pertaining to the presence and functioning of a component or a relevant principle, or if the components do not operate together in an integrated manner, the entity has an ineffective internal control system under the COSO framework.

Question 2	MCQ-09689

The Committee of Sponsoring Organizations' (COSO) *Internal Control—Integrated Framework* includes five distinct components that include all the following, *except*:

1. Control Environment
2. Risk Assessment
3. Risk Response
4. Control Activities

4 Enterprise Risk Management

In 2004, COSO issued *Enterprise Risk Management (ERM)—Integrated Framework* ("the framework") to assist organizations in developing a comprehensive response to risk management. In recognition of the changing complexity of risk, the emergence of new risks, and the enhanced awareness of risk management by both boards and executive oversight bodies, COSO published *Enterprise Risk Management—Integrating With Strategy and Performance* in 2017. The intent of ERM is to allow management to effectively deal with uncertainty, evaluate risk acceptance, and build value. The underlying premise of ERM is that every entity exists to provide value for stakeholders and that all entities face risk in the pursuit of value for its stakeholders. According to COSO, "Risk is the possibility that events will occur and affect the achievement of strategy and business objectives."

4.1 Themes

The ERM framework includes the following themes.

- ERM is defined by COSO as the *culture, capabilities*, and *practices, integrated with strategy-setting and performance,* that organizations rely on to *manage risk* in creating, preserving, and realizing *value.*

- Management decisions will impact the development of value including its *creation, preservation, erosion,* and *realization.*

- Mission vision and core values define what an entity strives to be and how it wants to conduct business.

- Core values correlate with culture.

- Mission and vision correlate with strategy and business objectives.

- Risk appetite represents the types and amounts of risk, on a broad level, that an organization is willing to accept in pursuit of value.

- ERM seeks to align risk appetite and strategy.

- Application of ERM is intended to provide management with a reasonable expectation of success with:

  - Enhancement of risk response decisions

  - Identification and management of multiple and cross-enterprise risks

  - Seizing opportunities

  - Improving the deployment of capital

4.2 Objectives

ERM evaluates risk within the context of strategy and business objectives.

4.3 Components

The components of ERM follow in logical sequence using the mnemonic **GO PRO** and are supported by principles memorized as **DOVES SOAR VAPIR SIR TIP**.

4.3.1 **G**overnance and Culture

- Defines **D**esired culture
- Exercises board **O**versight
- Demonstrates commitment to core **V**alues
- Attracts, develops, and retains capable individuals (**E**mployees)
- Establishes operating **S**tructure

4.3.2 Strategy and **O**bjective-Setting

- Evaluates alternative **S**trategies
- Formulates business **O**bjectives
- **A**nalyzes business context
- Defines **R**isk appetite

4.3.3 **P**erformance

- Develops portfolio **V**iew
- **A**ssesses severity of risk (likelihood and impact)
- **P**rioritizes risk
- **I**dentifies risks (events)
- Implements risk **R**esponses (accept, pursue, reduce, share, or avoid)

4.3.4 **R**eview and Revision

- Assesses **S**ubstantial change
- Pursues **I**mprovement in Enterprise Risk Management
- **R**eviews risk and performance

4.3.5 Information, Communications, and Reporting (**O**ngoing)

- Leverages information and **T**echnology
- Communicates risk **I**nformation
- Reports on risk culture and **P**erformance

4.4   Limitations

Although ERM is an outstanding tool, its limitations include being subject to human judgment, evaluations made in error, and management override.

Question 3   MCQ-09691

Using COSO's *Enterprise Risk Management—Integrated Framework* as a basis for dealing with uncertainty while seeking profit and growth, an organization would:

1. Avoid all risk
2. Develop strategy in a manner that aligns with management's risk appetite
3. Only set entity-wide strategic goals
4. Eliminate uncertainty

II Economic Concepts and Analysis

A Economic and Business Cycles

B Market Influences on Business

C Financial Risk Management

1 Business Cycles

1.1 Components of the Business Cycle

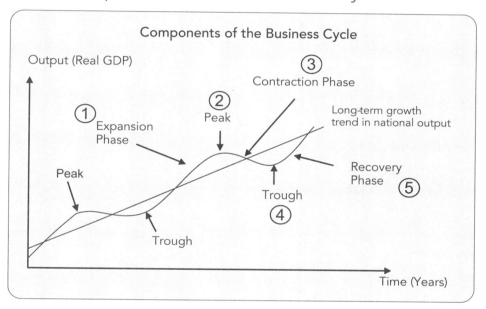

Components of the Business Cycle

Output (Real GDP)

③ Contraction Phase

② Peak

① Expansion Phase

Long-term growth trend in national output

Peak

Recovery Phase ⑤

Trough

Trough ④

Time (Years)

1.2 Economic Indicators

▪ Leading indicators tend to predict economic activity. Orders for goods would represent a leading indicator.

▪ Lagging indicators follow economic activity. Consumer price index for services would be a lagging indicator.

▪ Coincident indicators change at generally the same time as the whole economy. Industrial production (GDP) would represent a coincident indicator.

Question 1   MCQ-09189

Which component of the business cycle is characterized by falling economic activity and growth?

1. Expansionary phase.

2. Trough.

3. Contractionary phase.

4. Recovery phase.

2 Market Structures

Market structure refers to the type of market within which firms operate.

2.1 Perfect Competition

- A large number of firms
- Very little product differentiation
- No barriers to entry
- Firms are price takers

2.2 Monopolistic Competition

- A relatively large number of firms
- Differentiated products sold by the firms in the market
- Few barriers to entry
- Firm has control over quantity produced with price set by the market

2.3 Oligopoly

- Very few firms selling differentiated products
- Fairly significant barriers to entry
- Firms are interdependent (i.e., the actions of one firm affect the actions of other firms)
- Firms face kinked demand curves (match price cuts; ignore price increases).

2.4 Monopoly

- A single firm in a market
- Significant barriers to entry
- No substitute products for the good
- The ability of a firm to set output and prices

Question 2   MCQ-09112

In a perfectly competitive market, firms are likely to:

1. Devote significant resources to promote product differentiation.
2. Face significant barriers to market entry.
3. Match price cuts by competitors but ignore price increases.
4. None of the answer choices are correct.

---

3 Impact of Government Policies

A government's policies and actions can have a significant impact on industries. An industry and its entities can be positively or negatively affected by fiscal policy, monetary policy, regulation, and trade controls.

3.1   Fiscal Policy

Government spending and taxation can influence the economy.

- **Expansionary Fiscal Policy:** More government spending and lowered taxes stimulate the economy to expand.

- **Contractionary Fiscal Policy**: Reduced government spending and/or increased taxes are designed to slow economic growth and reduce inflation.

3.2   Monetary Policy

A nation's central bank (the Federal Reserve in the United States) uses monetary policy to stimulate or dampen the economy. The three tools used to implement monetary policy are open market operations, changes in the discount rate, and changes in the required reserve ratio.

- **Expansionary Monetary Policy:** By buying government securities and/ or decreasing the discount rate and the required reserve ratio, a central bank increases the money supply, which expands the economy.

- **Contractionary Monetary Policy:** By selling government securities and/ or increasing the discount rate and the required reserve ratio, a central bank decreases the money supply, which contracts the economy.

3.3   Regulations

Government establishes regulations that guide how an industry and its entities can operate. Examples of regulations include taxes, antitrust laws, and employment and labor laws.

3.4   Trade Controls

Trade controls restrict transactions and transfers of goods, services, software, and technology. Traditional trade controls include tariffs, quotas, and embargoes. Although trade controls can protect domestic industries, they also limit free trade and potentially harm the world economy.

Question 3	MCQ-09161

Which of the following is an example of expansionary fiscal policy?

1. A decrease in the required reserve ratio.

2. An increase in the discount rate.

3. A decrease in government spending.

4. A decrease in taxes.

Market Influences on Business

1 Demand

1.1 Fundamental Law of Demand

Fundamental law of demand states that the price of a product/service and the quantity demanded of that product/service are inversely related due to the:

- **Substitution Effect:** Consumers tend to purchase more (less) of a good when its price falls (rises) in relation to the price of other goods.
- **Income Effect:** When prices are lowered (income kept constant), consumers will purchase more of the lowered-price products.

1.2 Factors That Shift the Demand Curve

Factors that shift demand curves include changes in:

- Wealth
- Price of related goods (substitutes and complements)
- Consumer income
- Consumer tastes or product preferences
- Consumer expectations
- Number of buyers served by the market

2 Supply

2.1 Fundamental Law of Supply

Fundamental law of supply states that price and quantity supplied are positively related.

2.2 Factors That Shift the Supply Curve

Factors that shift supply curves include changes in:

- Price expectations of supplying firm
- Product costs
- Price or demand of other goods
- Subsidies or taxes
- Product technology

3 Market Equilibrium

3.1   Equilibrium Price and Output

A market's equilibrium price and output (quantity) is the point on the graph (next page) where the supply and demand curves intersect. This is also called the market's clearing price.

3.2   Changes in Equilibrium

■ When the demand curve shifts right, equilibrium price and quantity will increase.

■ When the demand curve shifts left, equilibrium price and quantity will fall.

■ When the supply curve shifts right, equilibrium price will fall and equilibrium quantity will increase (i.e., more of the good will be produced and sold at a lower price).

■ When the supply curve shifts left, equilibrium price will increase and equilibrium quantity will fall.

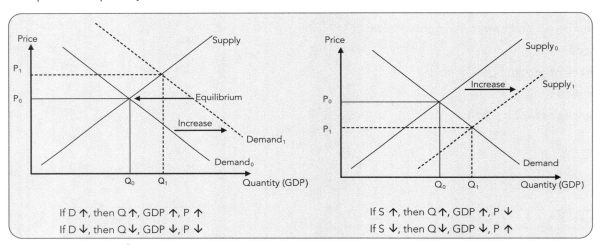

If D ↑, then Q ↑, GDP ↑, P ↑	If S ↑, then Q ↑, GDP ↑, P ↓
If D ↓, then Q ↓, GDP ↓, P ↓	If S ↓, then Q ↓, GDP ↓, P ↑

Question 1   MCQ-09082

Which of the following events would lead to an increase in the equilibrium price of a good and a decrease in the equilibrium quantity?

1. A decrease in consumer income.

2. An increase in production costs.

3. An increase in the price of a substitute good.

4. A decrease in the price of a complementary good.

Question 2   MCQ-09195

When the supply curve shifts to the left:

1. Equilibrium price and quantity will rise.
2. Equilibrium price and quantity will fall.
3. Equilibrium price will rise and equilibrium quantity will fall.
4. Equilibrium price will fall and equilibrium quantity will rise.

4 Elasticity

4.1 Price Elasticity of Demand

$$\text{Price elasticity of demand} = \frac{\text{\% Change in quantity demanded}}{\text{\% Change in price}}$$

- Inelastic demand (Price elasticity of demand < 1.0)
- Elastic demand (Price elasticity of demand > 1.0)
- Unit elastic demand (Price elasticity of demand = 1.0)

4.2 Price Elasticity of Supply

$$\text{Price elasticity of supply} = \frac{\text{\% Change in quantity supplied}}{\text{\% Change in price}}$$

- Inelastic supply (Price elasticity of supply < 1.0)
- Elastic supply (Price elasticity of supply > 1.0)
- Unit elastic supply (Price elasticity of supply = 1.0)

4.3 Cross Elasticity and Income Elasticity of Demand

4.3.1 Cross Elasticity

Per the formula below, a positive coefficient indicates substitute goods, whereas a negative coefficient indicates complement goods.

$$\text{Cross elasticity of demand (supply)} = \frac{\text{\% Change in number of units of X demanded (supplied)}}{\text{\% Change in price of Y}}$$

4.3.2   Income Elasticity of Demand

Per the formula below, if the income elasticity of demand is positive then the good is a normal good, whereas if the income elasticity of demand is negative then the good is an inferior good.

$$\text{Income elasticity of demand (supply)} = \frac{\%\ \text{Change in number of units of X demanded (supplied)}}{\%\ \text{Change in income}}$$

Question 3

MCQ-09092

When the price of shrimp rises from $5 per pound to $6 per pound, the quantity demanded of shrimp falls from 100 pounds to 90 pounds. What is the price elasticity of demand for shrimp?

1. 0.10
2. 2.00
3. 0.50
4. 0.70

5 Effects of Inflation on the Economy

5.1 Effect of Inflation on Prices

A sustained increase in the general prices of goods and services decreases purchasing power. Entities holding monetary assets will suffer while entities holding monetary liabilities will benefit.

5.2 Effect of Inflation on Investments

Inflation erodes the purchasing power of fixed-coupon payments and the final principal payment which, therefore, reduces the present value of the investment. Unless adjusted for inflation, dividends or stock payouts from equity investments will also be eroded. Alternative investments can be an effective hedge against inflation.

5.3 Effect of Inflation on Future Expenses

In an inflationary environment, the costs of production will increase, requiring entities to increase sales prices to maintain profit margins. Entities that cannot contain costs or raise prices will suffer.

6 Developing and Implementing Strategy

6.1 Factors That Influence Strategy (SWOT)

- Internal factors (**s**trengths and **w**eaknesses)
- External factors (**o**pportunities and **t**hreats)

6.2 Porter's Five Forces Affecting Competition and Firm Profitability

- Barriers to market entry
- Market competitiveness
- Existence of substitute products
- Bargaining power of customers
- Bargaining power of suppliers

6.3   Types of Competitive Strategies

6.3.1   Cost Leadership Strategies

- Broad range of buyers
- Narrow range (niche) of buyers
- Successful in markets where buyers have large bargaining power and price competition exists

6.3.2   Differentiation Strategies

- Broad range of buyers
- Narrow range (niche) of buyers
- Successful in markets where customers see value in individual products

6.3.3   Best Cost Strategies

- Combines cost leadership and differentiation strategies
- Successful when generic products are not considered acceptable but customers are sensitive to value

6.3.4   Focus/Niche Strategies

- Focus is on satisfying a particular customer segment (niche)
- Successful when niche is large enough so that firm can generate a profit

---

Question 4   MCQ-09201

Sportin' Dude Water Craft markets a range of personal watercraft for use in the ocean, rivers, or lakes. The company has been quite successful, but it has noted a decline in sales since the discovery of the dreaded Bombay virus, an ear infection caused by microbes that have been discovered this year in rivers and lakes throughout North America. When Sportin' Dude prepares its strategic plan, it will likely identify the discovery of the microbe as a:

1. Strength.
2. Weakness.
3. Opportunity.
4. Threat.

Question 5 MCQ-09182

Rivington Corp. is reviewing its competitive strategy. It has been following a combined cost leadership/differentiation/vertical integration strategy for its general retail merchandise division, but that strategy has not been working too well and the company has been losing market share to national competitors. Which of the following statements is/are more than likely correct with respect to competitive strategies?

I. Cost leadership strategies typically focus on building market share and matching the prices of rival firms. A possible reason for the lack of success of Rivington's cost leadership strategy is that it has an outmoded warehousing and distribution system.

II. Differentiation strategies attempt to gain competitive advantage by creating the perception that products are superior to those of competitors. A possible reason for the lack of success of Rivington's differentiation strategy is that it implemented its strategy by advertising its "everyday low prices."

III. Vertical integration strategies attempt to control an entire supply chain. A possible reason for the lack of success of Rivington's strategy is that it had not acquired any of the companies in its supply chain.

1. I and II only are correct.
2. I and III only are correct.
3. I only is correct.
4. I, II, and III are correct.

7 International Business Operations

7.1 Motivations for International Business Operations

Economic theory supports international trade as a means of achieving improved shareholder value.

- **Comparative Advantage:** Specialization in the production and trade of specific products produces a comparative advantage in relation to trading partners.

- **Imperfect Markets:** To obtain more resources, companies must trade outside their borders.

- **Product Cycle:** Product cycle theory predicts that domestic success will result in domestic competition, encouraging the export of products or services. Foreign success will, in turn, promote foreign competition. The entity is then motivated to establish a business outside its boundaries to differentiate itself and to compete with foreign business rivals.

7.2 Methods of Conducting International Business Operations

Multinational operations can be structured in various ways. These include:

- **International Trade:** Companies and nations import and export products or services.
- **Licensing:** Entities provide the right to use processes or technologies in exchange for a fee.
- **Franchising:** Entities provide training and related service delivery resources in exchange for a fee.
- **Joint Ventures:** Taking advantage of comparative advantage of one or both of the participants in marketing or delivering a product.
- **Direct Foreign Investment (DFI):** An entity establishes international operations by purchasing a foreign company as a subsidiary or by starting a subsidiary operation within a foreign country.
- **Global Sourcing:** The synchronization of all levels of product manufacturing, including research and development, production, and marketing, on an international basis.

7.3 Relevant Factors of International Business Operations

Companies must consider many relevant factors when creating a global business strategy. These include:

- Political and legal influences
- Potential for asset expropriation
- Taxes and tariffs
- Limitations on asset ownership or joint venture participation
- Content or value-added limits
- Foreign trade zones
- Economic systems
- Culture

7.4 Risks of International Business Operations

Many risks arise from conducting international business operations.

- Exchange rate or currency risks arise as exchange rates fluctuate. Transaction risk, economic risk, and translation risk are the three types of exchange rate risk.
- The state of the foreign economy in which a company operates involves risks. Changes in demand, interest rates, inflation, and exchange rates in the foreign economy can have significant impacts.
- Political risks are noneconomic events or environmental conditions that are disruptive to financial operations. This includes barriers to trade, corruption, the host government's attitude toward foreign firms, consumer attitude toward foreign firms, and war.

8 Significant Business Transactions

8.1 Business Combinations

The primary types of business combinations include horizontal, vertical, circular, and diagonal combinations.

- A horizontal combination occurs when companies in the same industry join under single management.
- A vertical combination involves the combination of companies at different stages of the production.
- A circular combination occurs when different business units with relatively removed connections come together under single management.
- A diagonal combination occurs when a company that engages in an activity integrates with another company that provides ancillary support for that primary activity.

Common business transactions include mergers, acquisitions, consolidations, tender offers, purchases of assets, and management acquisitions.

- In a merger, two or more entities combine to form a single new corporation.
- The acquisition of one company by another involves no new company. Only the acquirer remains after the acquisition.
- In a tender offer, a company makes an offer directly to shareholders to buy the outstanding shares of another company at a specified price.
- A purchase-of-assets transaction occurs when a portion or all of the selling company's assets are purchased by the acquiring company, which may result in the dissolution of the selling company.

8.2 Divestiture

A divestiture involves the partial or full disposal of a component or business unit of a company. Divestiture transactions include sell-offs, spin-offs, and equity carve-outs.

- A sell-off is an outright sale of a subsidiary because there is a lack of synergy between the company and its subsidiary.
- A spin-off creates a new, independent company by separating a subsidiary business from a parent company.
- An equity carve-out occurs when a subsidiary is made public through an initial public offering, thereby creating a new publicly listed company.

9   Supply Chain Management

9.1   Supply Chain Operations Reference (SCOR) Model

- Plan
- Source
- Make
- Deliver

9.2   Benefits of Supply Chain Management

- Reduced inventory, warehousing, and packaging costs
- Reduction of delivery and transportation costs
- Improved service and delivery times
- Management and integration of suppliers
- Cross-docking (minimization of handling and storage costs)

1 Risk Definitions—Exposures to Loss

1.1 Interest Rate (Yield) Risk

Losses in underlying asset value or increases in underlying liability value as a result of changes in market interest rates.

1.2 Market Risk

Losses in trading value of asset or liability in markets. Market risk is nondiversifiable risk.

1.3 Credit Risk

Inability to secure debt financing in a timely and affordable manner.

1.4 Default Risk

The possibility that a debtor may not repay the principal or interest due on their debt obligation on a timely basis.

1.5 Liquidity Risk

The investor desires to sell a security but cannot do so on a timely basis or without material price concessions.

Question 1   MCQ-09223

Arbor Corporation is evaluating its working capital financing needs. Management is concerned about increasing interest rates and has elected to fund its working capital needs with an equity loan from Harbor National Bank collateralized by land. The Arbor Corporation's decision is most likely designed to minimize:

1. Interest rate risk.
2. Market risk.
3. Credit risk.
4. Default risk.

---

2 Computation of Return

2.1 Stated Interest Rate

The rate of interest charged before adjustments for compounding or market factors.

2.2 Effective Interest Rate

The actual finance charge associated with a borrowing after reducing the loan proceeds for charges and fees.

2.3 Simple Interest Rate

The amount of interest paid on the original principal without including compounding. The formula is: $SI = P_0(i)(n)$

2.4 Compound Interest

The amount of interest earnings or expense that is based on the original principal plus unpaid interest earnings or expense. The formula is:
$FV_n = P_0(1 + i)^n$

2.5 Required Rate of Return

Start with the risk-free rate and add the market risk premium, inflation premium, liquidity risk premium, and default risk premium.

Question 2 MCQ-09730

The required rate of return consists of which of the following?

1. Simple interest rate + compounding premium + market risk premium + inflation risk premium + default risk premium.
2. Effective interest rate + market risk premium + default risk premium.
3. Compound interest rate + default risk premium + market risk premium + inflation risk premium.
4. Risk-free rate + market risk premium + inflation premium + liquidity risk premium + default risk premium.

---

3 Financial Decisions Using Probability and Expected Value

3.1 Probability

Probability represents a chance (expressed as a percentage) that an event will occur, with a zero (0 percent) assigned when there is no chance an event will occur and a one (100 percent) assigned if there is complete certainty that an event will occur. For example, the probability of selecting an M from the 26 letters of the alphabet is 1 in 26 or 1/26.

3.2 Expected Value

Expected value is the weighted average of the probability assigned to each expected outcome of occurrence. For example, if the probability of selling 5,000 cars is 20 percent and the probability of selling 4,000 cars is 80 percent, the expected value is 4,200 cars [(80% × 4,000) + (20% × 5,000)].

4 Circumstances Creating Exchange Rate Fluctuations

Exchange rate fluctuations are generally caused by two factors.

4.1 Trade Factors

- Inflation rates
- Income levels
- Government controls

4.2 Financial Factors

- Interest rates
- Capital flows

Question 3   MCQ-09190

An international firm based in the United States is forecasting the impact of various factors on its trade in foreign markets. Each of the following factors would serve to improve the exchange rate of the U.S. dollar relative to foreign currencies, except:

1. Foreign inflation.
2. Declining domestic income.
3. Low foreign interest rates.
4. Increased foreign capital investment.

5 Risk Exposures Implied by Exchange Rate Fluctuations

5.1   Transaction Exposure

Dealing in foreign currencies exposes the parties involved to potential economic loss or gain upon settlement of a transaction in a foreign currency. (Note: This is either a purchase transaction resulting in a payable or a sales transaction resulting in a receivable.)

5.2   Economic Exposure

Exposure to economic risks related to exchange rate fluctuations pertains to the possibility that the value of cash flows could fluctuate up or down as a result of changes in the exchange rate.

The following diagram summarizes the relationship.

Assume: at $time_0 \rightarrow \$1 = €1$

	Receive € (Net inflows)	Paying € (Net outflows)
If U.S. $ appreciates to $0.75 = €1→	**1.** Loss	**2.** Gain
If U.S. $ depreciates to $1.25 = €1 →	**3.** Gain	**4.** Loss

Example

1. Company A has a €100 receivable. The U.S. $ appreciates from $1 = €1 to $0.75 = €1. Originally, once this €100 was received, it could be converted to $100 at the initial exchange rate. But, when the U.S. $ appreciates, the same €100 receivable can only be converted to $75 (loss).

2. If Company A had a payable of €100, originally it cost $100. But when the U.S. $ appreciates, the same €100 payable can be satisfied with $75 (gain).

3. If Company A has a €100 receivable and the U.S. $ depreciates from $1 = €1 to $1.25 = €1, once the €100 is received, it can be converted to €100 = $125 (gain).

4. If Company A has a €100 payable and the U.S. $ depreciates, to satisfy the €100 payable, it requires $125 instead of $100 (loss).

5.3   Translation Exposure

Translation exposure is the potential that the consolidation of the financial statements of domestic parents with foreign subsidiaries will result in changes in account balances and income as a result of exchange rate fluctuations. Translation exposure increases as the degree of involvement by the parent with international subsidiaries increases. This exposure is also affected by the stability of a foreign currency versus the parent currency, with a stable (unstable) foreign currency decreasing (increasing) translation risk. Translation exposure is also known as accounting exposure.

Question 4 — MCQ-09196

Shore Co. records its transactions in U.S. dollars. A sale of goods resulted in a receivable denominated in Japanese yen, and a purchase of goods resulted in a payable denominated in euros. Shore recorded a foreign exchange gain on collection of the receivable and an exchange loss on settlement of the payable. The exchange rates are expressed as so many units of foreign currency to one dollar. Did the number of foreign currency units exchangeable for a dollar increase or decrease between the contract and settlement dates?

	Yen exchangeable for $1	Euros exchangeable for $1
1.	Increase	Increase
2.	Decrease	Decrease
3.	Decrease	Increase
4.	Increase	Decrease

Question 5 — MCQ-09152

Hickman International is based in the United States, but it conducts significant business in Canada. The company's exposure to economic risks of exchange rate fluctuation include:

1. The potential that accounts receivable denominated in Canadian dollars may be exchanged for fewer United States dollars at the settlement date than on the date of origination.

2. The potential that net sales in Canadian markets (inflows) are denominated in a devalued currency that is less valuable than the United States dollar, thereby reducing the present value of the company.

3. The potential that the remeasurement of subsidiary financial statements denominated in Canadian dollars may produce a foreign exchange loss.

4. The potential that translated financial statements might reflect a reduction in comprehensive income.

6 Hedging to Mitigate Exchange Rate Transaction Exposure

Hedging is a financial risk management technique in which an entity, that is attempting to mitigate the risk fluctuations in exposure, acquires a financial instrument that behaves in the opposite manner from the hedged item. There are several hedging transactions that can be used by an entity to mitigate transaction exposure from both an accounts payable and accounts receivable application basis.

6.1 Futures Hedge

A futures hedge entitles the holder to either purchase or sell a number of currency units for a negotiated price on a stated date. Futures hedges are used for smaller amounts.

6.2 Forward Hedge

A forward hedge is similar to a futures hedge, but the owner of the contract is entitled to buy or sell volumes of currency at a point in time. Forward contracts identify groups of transactions for larger amounts.

6.3 Money Market Hedge

Money market hedges use foreign money markets to meet future cash flow needs and mitigate exchange rate risks by investment in financial institutions of the foreign economy. Money market hedges may be executed with either excess cash discounted and invested in the foreign economy or through simultaneous borrowing and reinvesting in the foreign economy.

6.4 Currency Option Hedge

Currency option hedges use the same principles as forward hedge contracts and money market hedge transactions, except the owner has the option (and not the obligation) to execute the hedge transaction. The acquisition of an option requires payment of consideration (a premium). The owner of the option must consider the cost of the premium as part of determining the value of exercising the option.

6.5 Long-Term Forward Contract

A long-term forward contract works like any other forward contract but is used to stabilize transaction exposure over long periods. An entity may use long-term forward contracts to hedge long-term purchase contracts.

6.6 Currency Swap

A currency swap can be used to mitigate transaction exposure for longer term transactions. For example, two firms may enter into a currency swap whereby the firms agree to swap their currencies received at a future date for a negotiated exchange rate.

Question 6   MCQ-09162

Siaggas International is a United States corporation with substantial dealings in Europe. The company is hedging the amounts it owes on individual accounts payable denominated in euros. The financial instrument most likely used by the company would be:

1. Futures contracts to buy the specific number of euros to settle the debt at the spot rate at the time the liability was incurred.

2. Futures contracts to sell the specific number of euros to settle the debt at the spot rate at the time the liability was incurred.

3. Forward contracts to buy the monthly requirement of euros to satisfy anticipated accounts payable for the month.

4. Forward contracts to sell the monthly requirement of euros to satisfy anticipated accounts payable for the month.

7 Hedging to Mitigate Economic and Translation Exposure

Economic and translation exposure to exchange rate fluctuations involves overall business planning and design which create potential exposures to cash flow (economic) or financial reporting (translation) risks related to exchange rate fluctuation.

7.1   Restructuring

Economic exposure to currency fluctuations can be mitigated by restructuring the sources of income and expense to the consolidated entity. A downside to restructuring is that it is usually more difficult to manage than ordinary hedges.

8 Transfer Pricing

The primary reason for developing transfer pricing arrangements between domestic parents and foreign subsidiaries is to minimize local taxation. Additionally, intercompany cash transfers are often managed through the use of a "leading" transfer policy (subsidiaries with strong cash position) or a "lagging" transfer policy (subsidiaries with weak cash position).

III Financial Management

A Capital Structure

B Working Capital

C Financial Valuation Methods

D Financial Decision Models

Notes

Business Final Review

Notes

Business Final Review

© Becker Professional Education Corporation. All rights reserved.

1 Factors Affecting Short-Term and Long-Term Financing

1.1 Short-Term Financing

Advantages of short-term financing include increased liquidity, higher profitability, and lower financing costs. Disadvantages of short-term financing are higher interest rate risk and reduced capital availability.

1.2 Long-Term Financing

Advantages of long-term financing are lower interest rate risk and increased capital availability. Disadvantages of long-term financing include reduced profitability, decreased liquidity, and higher financing costs.

2 Methods of Short-Term Financing

2.1 Working Capital Financing

Working capital financing entails current assets being financed with trade accounts payable and accrued liabilities.

2.2 Letter of Credit

A letter of credit is a third-party guarantee (e.g., a bank).

2.3 Line of Credit

A line of credit is a revolving line of short-term borrowing with a financial institution.

Cash Burn Enterprises is entering a period of intense cash utilization. The company is apprehensive about cash flow timing and ensuring consistent cooperation of its vendors to provide needed supplies. Management would likely use what short-term financing instruments or strategies to meet this challenge:

1. Letter of credit.
2. Line of credit.
3. Subordinated debentures.
4. Working capital financing.

3 Methods of Long-Term Financing

3.1 Leasing Options

When a lease commences, the lessee must determine whether the lease should be classified as an operating or finance lease.

3.1.1 Operating Leases

With an operating lease, the balance sheet of the lessee will reflect a right-of-use (ROU) asset and a lease liability. The ROU asset will be amortized while the lease liability will be paid down over the life of the lease. On the income statement, lease expense will be recognized each year over the lease term.

3.1.2 Finance Leases

Similar to an operating lease, with a finance lease the lessee will reflect both an ROU asset and a lease liability on its balance sheet. Each lease payment will consist of part interest and part principal paydown, with interest expense shown on the income statement and the reduction of the liability reflected on the balance sheet.

Note that lessees can make an accounting policy election and choose to not recognize ROU assets and lease liabilities for leases with terms of 12 months or less. This election must be done by class of underlying asset and cannot include purchase options for the asset that the lessee is reasonably certain to exercise.

3.2 Debentures and Bonds

Bonds are a form of indebtedness that obligates the borrower to pay an agreed coupon payment (usually semiannually) over a period of years.

3.2.1 Debentures

Debentures are unsecured bonds that are backed by the full faith and credit of the issuer.

3.2.2 Subordinated Debentures

Subordinated debentures are unsecured obligations that rank behind senior fixed-income securities in the event of an issuer liquidation.

3.2.3 Income Bonds

Income bonds are fixed-income securities that pay interest only upon achievement of target income levels.

3.2.4 Mortgage Bonds

Mortgage bonds are long-term loans that are secured by residential or commercial real property.

3.3 Equity Financing

3.3.1 Preferred Stock

Preferred stock is a hybrid security that has similar features to both debt and equity. Preferred shareholders usually receive a fixed dividend payment, and in the event of an issuer liquidation, rank higher than common stockholders in regard to the claim to the issuer's assets. Usually, preferred stockholders do not have voting rights.

3.3.2 Common Stock

Common stock is the basic equity ownership of a corporation. Although common stockholders may receive capital gains (in addition to periodic dividends) when holding the issuer's stock, they have a residual (last) claim to the issuer's assets in the event of a liquidation.

4 Debt Covenants

Creditors use debt covenants in their lending agreements to protect their interests by limiting or prohibiting the action of the debtor that might negatively affect the position of the creditors. Debt covenants can be positive (i.e., the issuer must provide periodic financial statements), negative (i.e., restriction on asset sales), or financial (i.e., minimum interest coverage ratio).

5 Leverage

5.1 Operating Leverage

- Operating leverage is the degree to which a firm uses fixed operating costs, as opposed to variable operating costs.
- A firm with significant operating leverage must have sufficient sales revenues to cover high fixed operating costs.
- Beyond breakeven, a firm with higher fixed costs will retain a higher percentage of additional revenues as operating income.

5.2 Financial Leverage

- Financial leverage is defined is the degree to which a firm uses debt (as opposed to equity) in its capital structure.
- A firm with significant financial leverage must have sufficient operating income (EBIT) to cover fixed interest costs.
- Once the interest costs are covered, additional EBIT goes straight to net income and earnings per share.

Question 2   MCQ-09720

Which of the following statements is true for both operating and financial leverage?

1. Financing the firm with a very high percentage of common stock relative to long-term debt is a technique used to achieve both financial and operating leverage.

2. Investors and firms both use leverage in an attempt to increase profits, although there is no guarantee this will happen.

3. Using a high degree of both types of leverage (financial and operating) is an excellent way to minimize risk.

4. Increasing variable operating expenses results in higher leverage for a manufacturing firm.

---

6 Cost of Capital Computations

6.1   Cost of Long-Term Debt

The after-tax cost of debt is the multiplication of the pretax cost of debt by one minus the tax rate, as follows:

6.1.1   After-Tax Cost of Debt

$$\text{After-tax cost of debt} = \text{Pretax cost of debt} \times (1 - \text{Tax rate})$$

$$= 0.125 \times (1 - 0.30)$$

$$= 0.125 \times 0.70$$

$$= 0.0875$$

The terms are defined as follows:

Pretax cost of debt = Face amount × Coupon rate [*Assumed to be 12.5%*]

(1 − Tax rate) = 1 minus tax rate stated as a decimal [*Tax rate assumed to be 30%*]

6.2   Cost of Equity Capital

6.2.1   Cost of Preferred Stock

$$\text{Cost of preferred stock} = \text{Preferred stock dividends} / \text{Net proceeds of preferred stock}$$

$$= 10 / (100 - 5)$$

$$= 10 / 95$$

$$= 0.10526$$

The terms are defined as follows:

Preferred stock dividends = Cash dividends on preferred stock [*Assumed to be $10 per share*]

Net proceeds of preferred stock = Proceeds of preferred stock sale net of fees and costs
[*Assumed to be $100 and $5 per share, respectively*]

A Capital Structure

6.2.2 Cost of Common Stock—Discounted Cash Flows (DCF) Method

Cost of common equity = (Expected dividend / Current stock price) + Constant growth rate in dividends

$$= (2.15 / 25.25) + 0.075$$

$$= 0.0851 + 0.075$$

$$= 0.1601$$

The assumed amounts are:

16.01% = Cost of common equity

$2.15 = Expected dividend

$25.25 = Current stock price

7.5% = Constant growth rate in dividends

6.3 Capital Asset Pricing Model (CAPM)

In addition to the DCF method shown above, the cost of retained earnings can be calculated using the capital asset pricing model (CAPM).

6.3.1 CAPM Formula for Cost of Retained Earnings

The CAPM formula may be expressed as:

Cost of retained earnings = Risk-free rate + Risk premium

$$= \text{Risk-free rate of return} + \left(\frac{\text{Beta coefficient}}{\text{of stock}} \times \frac{\text{Market}}{\text{risk premium}} \right)$$

$$= \text{Risk-free rate of return} + \left[\text{Beta coefficient of stock} \times \left(\frac{\text{Market}}{\text{rate}} - \frac{\text{Risk-free}}{\text{rate of return}} \right) \right]$$

$$= 0.05 + [1.2 \times (0.14 - 0.05)]$$

$$= 0.158$$

The assumed amounts are:

5% = Risk-free rate of return

1.2 = Beta coefficient of stock

9% = Market risk premium (14% − 5%)

14% = Market rate

6.4   Weighted Average Cost of Capital (WACC)

The weighted average cost of capital is the sum of the weighted percentage of each form of capitalization used by a business. The optimal cost of capital is the combination of debt and equity securities (debt to equity ratio) that produces the lowest weighted average cost of capital.

6.4.1   Formula

$$WACC = \left(\frac{E}{V}\right)(R_e) + \left(\frac{P}{V}\right)(R_p) + \left(\frac{D}{V}\right)\left[R_d(1-T)\right]$$

Where:

V = The summed market values of the individual components of the firm's capital structure: common stock equity (E), preferred stock equity (P), and debt (D)

R = The required rate of return (also known as the "cost") of the various components

T = The corporate tax rate

6.4.2   Optimal Cost of Capital

The following graph illustrates the relationship between the weighted average cost of capital and the relationship between the elements of an entity's capitalization (the debt-to-equity ratio).

A   Capital Structure

Question 3   MCQ-09085

Gibson Enterprises issued 1,000 of its 8%, $50 par value preferred shares for $52 per share and incurred $2,500 in flotation costs. What was Gibson's cost of preferred stock?

1. 8.42%
2. 8.08%
3. 8.00%
4. 7.69%

Question 4   MCQ-09095

SmallCap Corp. is a relatively new company whose limited number of low-cost shares are actively traded on the NASDAQ. The value of the company's shares is fairly volatile and has fluctuated by 25% more than the overall fluctuation of the values of the total exchange. The expected return on the market is 12%. The company has the cash from accumulated earnings necessary for its expansion and currently has the funds in highly liquid, risk-free, federally insured securities yielding 2%. Management has elected to use the capital asset pricing model (CAPM) to compute its cost of capital to assist in evaluating financing alternatives. What is the cost of capital using the CAPM?

1. 2.00%
2. 12.00%
3. 14.50%
4. 10.00%

1   Debt Ratios

1.1   Solvency

Solvency is a measure of security for long-term creditors/investors.

$$\text{Debt-to-equity ratio} = \frac{\text{Total liabilities}}{\text{Total equity}}$$

$$\text{Total debt ratio} = \frac{\text{Total liabilities}}{\text{Total assets}}$$

2   Working Capital Ratios

2.1   Liquidity

Liquidity measures a firm's short-term ability to meet its current obligations.

$$\text{Current ratio} = \frac{\text{Current assets}}{\text{Current liabilities}}$$

$$\text{Quick ratio} = \frac{\text{Cash and cash equivalents} + \text{Short-term marketable securities} + \text{Receivables (net)}}{\text{Current liabilities}}$$

3   Cash Management Strategies

Cash management objectives include fee reduction, expediting deposits, and fraud protection.

3.1   Fee Reduction

3.1.1   Compensating Balances

Bank fees are waived when the customer maintains minimum account balances.

3.1.2   Trade Credit

Trade credit maximizes the availability of funding with no (or reduced) charges.

3.1.3 Commercial Paper

Commercial paper is a source of short-term financing by the issuer and an investment of idle cash by the buyer.

3.2 Expedite Deposits

3.2.1 Zero-Balance Account

The zero-balance account maintains a zero balance at all times. Its use reduces the elapsed time for transfers between accounts and maximizes availability of idle cash.

3.2.2 Electronic Fund Transfers (EFTs)

Electronic fund transfers allow for direct deposit of funds.

3.2.3 Lockbox System

With a lockbox system, customers send payments to a PO box or a location accessible by the bank.

3.3 Fraud Protection

Official bank checks (aka depository transfer checks) are designed to insulate the company from fraud and simplify bookkeeping.

Question 1   MCQ-09076

A cash manager trying to increase the availability of cash would likely use any one of the following techniques or banking services, except:

1. Compensating balance arrangements.
2. Zero-balance account arrangements.
3. Electronic funds transfer agreements.
4. Lock box systems.

---

4 Cash Discounts Used in Credit Terms

Different elements of working capital can be used to manage current position.

4.1 Accounts Payable

Cash discounts are frequently offered for early payment of accounts payable or receivable. The terms are stated with the percentage discount available if paid within a discount period along with the full term of the obligation. The term "2/10, net 30" indicates that payment within 10 days will earn a 2 percent discount, but that the full payment is due within 30 days. The cost of discounts not taken can be calculated using the following steps:

1. Compute the number of times the discount-forgone period occurs in a year:

> Days per year ÷ Days outstanding after discount
>
> For terms 2/10, net 30:
>
> 360 days per year ÷ (30 days term − 10 days discount) = 360 ÷ 20 = 18

2. Compute the effective interest rate associated with discount forgone:

> Discount % offered ÷ (100% − Discount % offered)
>
> For terms 2/10, net 30:
>
> 2% ÷ (100% − 2%) = 0.020408

3. Annualize by multiplying the effective rate by the number of times the discount-forgone period occurs in a year:

> 0.020408 × 18 times = 36.7%

Question 2   MCQ-09146

Cable Services Corporation offers cash discounts to its customers at terms of 2/12 net 30. Assuming a 360-day year, the maximum annualized interest rate Cable would earn from customers who elect to forgo the discount opportunity and pay at the end of the term would be:

1. 24.0%
2. 36.7%
3. 40.8%
4. 61.2%

---

5   Operating and Cash Conversion Cycles

5.1   Operating Cycle

The length of time from the initial expenditure until the time the cash is collected from customers. The operating cycle is calculated by adding the days in inventory to the days sales in accounts receivable.

5.1.1   Inventory Turnover Ratio

The inventory turnover ratio measures the number of times over an accounting period that inventory is sold.

$$\text{Inventory turnover} = \frac{\text{Cost of goods sold}}{\text{Average inventory}}$$

5.1.2   Days in Inventory

The average number of days inventory is held before it is sold.

$$\text{Days in inventory} = \frac{\text{Ending inventory}}{\text{Cost of goods sold} / 365}$$

5.1.3   Receivables Turnover

Receivables turnover measures the number of times receivables are collected over an accounting period (typically one year).

$$\text{Accounts receivable turnover} = \frac{\text{Sales (net)}}{\text{Average accounts receivable (net)}}$$

5.1.4   Days Sales in Accounts Receivable

The average number of days after a typical credit sale is made until the firm receives payment.

$$\text{Days sales in accounts receivable} = \frac{\text{Ending accounts receivable (net)}}{\text{Sales (net)} / 365}$$

5.2   Cash Conversion Cycle

The cash conversion cycle, or net operating cycle, adjusts the operating cycle for the time in which vendors are paid by the firm for the initial expenditure. The cash conversion cycle takes the operating cycle and subtracts the days of payables outstanding.

5.2.1   Accounts Payable Turnover

Accounts payable turnover measures the number of times payables are paid by the firm over an accounting period.

$$\text{Accounts payable turnover} = \frac{\text{Cost of goods sold}}{\text{Average accounts payable}}$$

5.2.2   Days of Payables Outstanding

The average number of days a firm takes to pay its vendors for purchases made on credit.

$$\text{Days of payables outstanding} = \frac{\text{Ending accounts payable}}{\text{Cost of goods sold} / 365}$$

Question 3   MCQ-09116

XYZ Corporation had net sales of $730,000 for the year ended December 31, Year 3, up over 8% from prior year levels of $675,000. The company has experienced a nearly 15% increase in accounts receivable from $41,000 at December 31, Year 2, to $47,000 at December 31, Year 3. Management wants to know if the days sales in accounts receivable for the current year has deteriorated from prior year levels of under 21 days. What is the days sales in accounts receivable for the year ended December 31, Year 3?

1. 16.59
2. 22.00
3. 22.86
4. 23.50

6 Accounts Receivable

Accounts receivable can be sold (factored) to expedite cash collections. Factors will typically charge a fee on all receivables purchased, as well as interest on cash given in advance to the seller prior to the factor collecting from the seller's customers.

7 Inventory Management Techniques

Inventory management techniques focus on maintaining the minimum quantities on hand necessary to meet current needs.

7.1 Just-in-Time

A just-in-time inventory system reduces the lag time between inventory arrival and inventory use. It assumes zero defects.

7.2 Economic Order Quantity (EOQ)

Economic order quantity formulates the order size that will minimize both ordering costs and carrying costs.

$$EOQ = \sqrt{\frac{2SO}{C}}$$

The terms are defined as follows:

EOQ = Economic order quantity

S = Annual sales in units

O = Cost per purchase order (primarily production set-up costs)

C = Carrying cost per unit

Question 4   MCQ-09096

Efficiency Emporiums owns retail outlets exclusively devoted to the
marketing and distribution of closet organizers that it purchases
wholesale from a supplier. The company will sell 2,500 units in
the coming year. The company has estimated that the cost of a
purchase order is $1,000, the per unit cost of carrying a unit of
product in inventory is $500, and that the stock-out costs associated
with inventory is $25,000. What is the optimal inventory order for
Efficiency Emporiums?

  1. 100
  2. 120
  3. 208
  4. 240

Notes

1 Valuation Methods

Traditional financial valuation is based on the formula for the present value of an annuity. The formula is somewhat complex, but is applied in various forms throughout the financial management topic. Alternative valuation methods use variations of the price earnings (P/E) ratio. It is important to understand the valuation formulas, the implied assumptions of the formulas, and the effect of the behavior of financial managers on the evaluation of those assumptions.

2 Calculating the Present Value of an Annuity

2.1 Formula

Annuity present value $= C \times (1 - \text{Present value factor} / r)$

$$= C \times \{(1 - [1 / (1 + r)^t]) / r\}$$

The terms are defined as follows:

C = Cash annuity payment

r = Rate of return

t = Number of years

2.2 Assumptions

Key assumptions include the:

- Recurring amount of the annuity
- Appropriate discount rate
- Duration of the annuity
- Timing of the annuity

3 Perpetuities (Zero Growth Stock)

When a company is expected to pay the same dividend each period, the perpetuity formula can be used to determine the value of the company's stock. The formula (below) implies that the stock price will not increase because the dividend does not increase.

3.1   Per Share Valuation

Present value of a perpetuity = Stock value per share = $P = D/R$

The terms are defined as follows:

P = Price

D = Dividend

R = Required return

3.2   Assumptions

Key assumptions include:

- The dividend (and assume it will never change)
- The required return

4 Constant Growth (Dividend Discount Model)

If dividends are assumed to grow at a constant rate, the Gordon (constant) growth model can be used to determine the intrinsic (true) value of the company's stock.

4.1   Per Share Valuation With Assumed Growth

Stock value per share with assumed growth = $P_t = D_{(t+1)} / (R - G)$

The terms are defined as follows:

$$P_t = \text{Current price (price at period "t")}$$
$$D_{(t+1)} = \text{Dividend one year after period "t"}$$
$$R = \text{Required return}$$
$$G = \text{(Sustainable) Growth rate}$$

4.2 Assumptions

Key assumptions include:

- The calculation of dividends one year beyond the year in which you are determining the price.
- A required rate of return.
- A constant dividend growth rate.
- The formula implies that the stock price will grow at the same rate as the dividend, which is not unreasonable, especially for a mature company.

5 Price Multiples

5.1 Price-Earnings (P/E) Ratio

The P/E ratio, once calculated, can be applied to expected earnings (E_1) in order to determine the current stock price. It requires that earnings be greater than zero.

$$\text{P/E Ratio} = P_0/E_1$$

The terms are defined as follows:

$$P_0 = \text{Price or value today}$$
$$E_1 = \text{Expected earnings in one year}$$

5.2   PEG Ratio

The PEG ratio is a measure that demonstrates the effect of earnings growth on a company's P/E, assuming a linear relationship between P/E and growth.

$$PEG = \left[(P_0 / E_1) / G \right]$$
$$\text{Value of equity } (P_0) = PEG \times E_1 \times G$$

The terms are defined as follows:

P_0 = Price or value of stock today

E_1 = Expected earnings in one year

G = Growth rate = $100 \times$ Expected growth rate

5.3   Price-to-Sales Ratio

This price multiple can also be used to determine the intrinsic value of stock. The rationale for using this multiple is that sales are less subject to manipulation than earnings and sales can be used to generate a meaningful multiple even when the company's earnings are negative.

$$P / S = P_0 / S_1$$
$$\text{Value of equity } (P_0) = \left[P_0 / S_1 \right] \times S_1$$

The terms are defined as follows:

P_0 = Price or stock value today

S_1 = Expected sales in one year

5.4   Price-to-Cash Flow Ratio

The price-to-cash flow ratio is another multiple that can be used to calculate a stock's intrinsic value. This multiple may be preferred over P/E because cash flows are more difficult to manipulate than earnings and empirical evidence indicates that the P/CF multiple is more stable than the P/E ratio.

$$P / CF = P_0 / CF_1$$
$$\text{Value of equity } (P_0) = (P_0 / CF_1) \times CF_1$$

The terms are defined as follows:

> P_0 = Price or stock value today
>
> CF_1 = Expected cash flow in one year

5.5 Price-to-Book Ratio

The price-to-book ratio may be used to value a stock's intrinsic value. Unlike the prior multiples that focus on the income statement or the cash flow statement, the P/B ratio focuses on the balance sheet (common shareholders' equity).

> $$P / B = P_0 / B_0$$
>
> $$\text{Value of equity } (P_0) = (P_0 / B_0) \times B_0$$

The terms are defined as follows:

> P_0 = Price or stock value today
>
> B_0 = Book value of common equity

5.6 Assumptions

Price multiple ratios have similar assumption requirements, which can be influenced by management behaviors, including:

- Future earnings
- Future cash flows
- Future sales
- Future growth rate
- Duration of sales or earnings trends

6 Discounted Cash Flow Analysis (DCF)

Discounted cash flow analysis attempts to determine the intrinsic value of a stock by determining the present value of its expected future cash flows. DCF models used by analysts to perform an absolute valuation on an equity security include the dividend discount model (DDM), the free cash flow to equity (FCFE) model, and the free cash flow to the firm (FCFF) model.

7 Evaluating Assumptions Used in Valuations

Forecasting methods have numerous subjective elements that are subject to behavioral influences. These influences generally include:

7.1 Generalized Rules of Thumb

Generalized rules of thumb distort objective evaluation of evidence.

- Tendency to use stereotyped characterizations
- Use adjustments from presumed baselines
- Use of intuition rather than analysis

7.2 Behavior Biases

- Excessive optimism
- Confirmation bias
- Overconfidence
- Illusion of control

7.3 Effect of Loss Aversion

- Losses are more distracting than gains
- Managers are generally averse to sure losses

Question 1	MCQ-09731

Financial valuation of securities and companies can be accomplished with a number of different models, such as discounted cash flow, Gordon constant growth model, price/earnings multiples, etc. For all of them, varying assumptions are made, some of which are objective and some of which are subjective. Influences on the subjective assumptions can include all of the following except which one?

1. Generalized rules of thumb, which distort objective evaluation of evidence by the tendency to use stereotyped characterizations and adjustments from presumed baselines.

2. Behavioral biases, such as excessive optimism and overconfidence.

3. The effect of loss aversion, meaning managers are generally averse to sure losses.

4. The risk-free rate and volatility of the stock prices are constant over the option's life.

Question 2   MCQ-09185

Financial decisions are often influenced by behavioral factors. Which of the following is generally considered most distracting:

1. Overconfidence
2. Business losses
3. Use of available data
4. Excessive optimism

8 Models for Valuing Options

8.1 Valuing Options—Black-Scholes Model

A number of different factors enter into the determination of the value of an option. A commonly used method for option valuation is the Black-Scholes model. The calculation itself is extremely complex and most likely beyond the scope of the CPA Exam.

However, you do need a high-level understanding of the concepts and assumptions that underlie Black-Scholes. Accountants may use this method in valuing stock options when accounting for share-based payments. Option price calculators are widely available, so you do not need to understand the complexity of the actual calculations to apply this method.

8.2 Black-Scholes Model Inputs— Determinants of Option Value

▪ Current price of the underlying stock (higher price = higher option value)

▪ Option exercise price

▪ Risk-free interest rate (higher rate = higher option value)

▪ Current time until expiration (longer time = higher option value)

▪ Some measure of risk for the underlying stock (higher risk = higher option value)

▪ The dividend on the optioned stock (higher dividend = higher option value)

8.3 Assumptions

▪ Stock prices behave randomly.

▪ The risk-free rate and volatility of the stock prices are constant over the option's life.

▪ There are no taxes or transaction costs.

- The stock pays no dividends, although the model can be adapted to dividend-paying stock.
- The options are European-style (exercisable only at maturity).
- An option may or may not have value.

8.4 Limitations of the Black-Scholes Model

Despite its current use, the Black-Scholes model does have several limitations:

- Due to the model's assumptions, results generated from the Black-Scholes model may differ from real prices.
- It assumes instant, cost-less trading, which is unrealistic in today's markets.
- The model tends to underestimate extreme price movements.
- The model is not applicable to pricing American-style options.

1 Tax Effects of Decisions

After-tax cash flows are used in capital budgeting models.

1.1 After-Tax Costs and Benefits

1.1.1 After-Tax Costs

The formula for computing an after-tax cost follows:

> (1.00 − Tax rate)* × Tax-deductible cash expense = After-tax cost (Net cash outflow)
>
> * Complement of tax rate

1.1.2 After-Tax Benefits

The formula for computing an after-tax benefit follows:

> (1.00 − Tax rate)* × Taxable cash receipt = After-tax benefit (Net cash inflow)
>
> * Complement of tax rate

1.2 Depreciation Tax Shield

Even though depreciation does not directly affect cash flows, it does reduce the amount of income tax a company will pay: this effect is called a depreciation tax shield.

1.2.1 Formula

The formula for computing the tax shield follows:

> Tax rate × Depreciation expense = Depreciation tax shield

Question 1   MCQ-09165

PV Corporation (PVC) is evaluating an investment with an annual $150,000 pretax cash inflow for the next five years. The project will require additional working capital of $35,000. The tax rate is 35% and the anticipated additional depreciation for the project is $50,000. The company's hurdle rate is 8% and the related annuity and present value of $1 factors are as follows:

Present value of an annuity at 8% for 5 years	3.9927
Present value of $1 at 8% for 5 years	0.6806

ABC would compute first-year annual after-tax cash flows associated with the program at:

1. 100,000
2. 115,000
3. 130,000
4. 459,160

2 Discounted Cash Flow

Discounted cash flow (DCF) valuation methods (including the net present value and the internal rate of return methods discussed below) are techniques that use time value of money concepts to measure the present value of cash inflows and cash outflows expected from a project.

2.1 Factors

The following elements must be known:

- Dollar amount of initial investment.
- Rate of return desired for the project (discount rate).
- Dollar amount of future cash inflows and outflows (net of related income tax effects).

3 Net Present Value (NPV)

The net present value approach is generally thought to be the best technique to evaluate capital projects.

3.1 Characteristics

Net present value computations are based upon amounts (not percentages). The net present value method displays the net amount by which the present value of cash inflows exceeds (or does not exceed) the invested amount.

3.2 Formula

Discounted cash flows	$XXX
Less: Investment	<XXX>
NPV	XXX

3.3 Conclusions

Positive NPV indicates that the proposed investment exceeds the hurdle (minimum) rate and the investment should be considered. Investments that have a negative NPV should be rejected. A zero NPV indicates the proposed investment is expected to yield the exact hurdle rate of return.

3.4 Capital Rationing and the Profitability Index

3.4.1 Unlimited Capital

Pursue all investment options with a positive NPV.

3.4.2 Limited Capital

Allocate capital to the combination of projects with the maximum NPV.

3.4.3 Profitability Index

A means of ranking projects based on NPV.

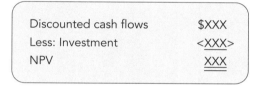

$$\text{Profitability index} = \frac{\text{Present value of net future cash inflow}}{\text{Present value of net initial investment}}$$

The higher this index is, the higher the expected NPV.

Question 2

Exeter Corporation has the opportunity to make a $150,000 capital investment that management anticipates will produce a $40,000 after-tax income stream in each of the next five years. The investment will have a 10% salvage value after taxes at the end of year five. The company's tax rate is 25% and the company's hurdle rate is 10%. What is the net present value of this investment given the following present value factors at 10%?

	Present Value of $1.00	Present Value of an Annuity
Year 1	0.909	0.909
Year 2	0.826	1.736
Year 3	0.751	2.487
Year 4	0.683	3.170
Year 5	0.621	3.791

1. ($1,600)
2. $1,600
3. $9,315
4. $10,955

4   Internal Rate of Return (IRR)

4.1   Characteristics

The internal rate of return method computes the percentage rate of return on a specific investment for comparison to a company's target (hurdle) rate of return. The internal rate of return produces a NPV equal to zero.

4.2   Limitations

Internal rate of return computations are less reliable than net present value computations when the investment alternative has variable cash flows. The IRR computation assumes the reinvestment of earnings at the IRR, a rate that may be unrealistic. In the absence of a financial calculator, interpolation and trial and error are required in order to calculate the IRR (unlikely on the exam).

5 Payback Methods

Payback methods may use either discounted or undiscounted approaches. The methods compute the number of years it will take to recoup the original investments.

5.1   Undiscounted Payback

5.1.1   Characteristics

Payback methods are based upon periods of time, not amounts of dollars or percentage returns.

$$\frac{\text{Investment}}{\text{Average annual cash flows}} = \text{Payback period}$$

5.1.2   Objectives and Limitations

The undiscounted payback method ignores profitability and the time value of money.

5.2   Discounted Payback

The discounted payback method is identical to the undiscounted method, except the after-tax cash flows are discounted in the computation for the number of years.

Question 3   MCQ-09135

Inexacta Enterprises wants to compute the payback on a $100,000 capital investment that is projected to produce $23,850 in after-tax cash inflows each year for the next five years and has a 7% salvage value at the end of the fifth year. What is the payback period in years?

1. 3.90
2. 4.19
3. 4.49
4. 5.93

Notes

IV Information Technology

A Information Technology (IT) Governance

B The Role of IT in Business

C Data Management and Analytics

D System Development and Change Management

E IT Risks and Responses

Notes

Information Technology (IT) Governance

1 The Importance of IT Governance

Information technology (IT) governance is a formal structure for how organizations align IT and business strategies. An IT governance framework should align key questions, metrics, and returns to the business.

IT governance is concerned with the strategic alignment between goals and objectives of the business and the utilization of its IT resources to effectively achieve the desired results.

2 Understanding and Defining IT Governance

IT governance establishes chains of responsibility, authority, and communication. It also establishes policies, standards, and control mechanisms to enable personnel within an organization to carry out their roles and responsibilities.

2.1 Key Principles for Governing IT

IT governance needs to be comprehensive and dynamic. Technology evolves at a rapid pace; therefore, an effective IT governance framework must be able to adapt while consistently meeting stakeholder needs. A strong data governance model will have the following components:

- **Availability:** Information must be available to the right employees at the right time.
- **Architecture:** Applications should be designed to meet governance objectives.
- **Metadata:** Data describing other data must be robust in terms of breadth and specificity.
- **Policy:** Data governance works to translate management objectives into practice.
- **Quality:** This means there are no missing values, duplicate values, transposed values, or mismatched records.
- **Regulatory Compliance and Privacy:** Information that is considered personally identifiable information (PII) should be secure by policies designed to ensure no violations of privacy laws.
- **Security:** IT governance should ensure the secure preservation, storage, and transmission of data.

An IT governance framework allows organizations to accommodate rapidly changing technology while also meeting stakeholders' needs. Two common frameworks are COSO's *Internal Control—Integrated Framework* and ISACA's Control Objectives for Information and Related Technology (COBIT) framework.

3 Aligning IT Governance With Organizational Objectives

IT governance practices allow an organization to achieve its goals and objectives as described in its overall vision and strategy.

3.1   Vision

A company's vision represents its aspirations and goals and is typically described in a vision statement. IT governance policies should be designed to facilitate the achievement of that vision.

3.2   Corporate Strategy

A corporate strategy shapes an organization's operations and business model. Corporate strategy must be supported by an appropriate IT strategy and IT governance.

3.3   IT Strategy

IT strategy should align with corporate strategy to achieve its objectives. The following IT factors may affect a company's corporate strategy:

- Network design
- Cybersecurity
- Disaster recovery and business continuity
- Available IT personnel

4 Structuring and Executing IT Governance

Effective IT governance requires participation from all levels of an organization. In addition, a well-functioning IT governance structure has the right policies and procedures in place to remain relevant, provide oversight, and align with organization goals.

4.1   People

- The board of directors is responsible for setting governance policies.
- Executives ensure that an IT governance structure is in place and executed effectively.
- Middle management is responsible for carrying out governance policies.
- IT support staff include network engineers, help desk, and cybersecurity staff.
- Accountants play an important role handling confidential information.

- End users are responsible for following processes and procedures.
- Customers and vendors affect how organizations utilize online commerce platforms.
- Auditors and regulators may drive changes in IT governance to comply with changing regulations.

4.2 Processes for Governance Execution

Governance teams must be well-positioned to assess and evaluate an organization's needs, direct management to address those needs, and effectively monitor the outcomes on a continuous basis.

- Project development teams monitor projects, manage the human element (resistance to change), communicate with users, and manage risk and escalating issues that cannot be resolved within the team.
- Steering committees develop and communicate strategic goals; review the IT budget and the allocation of IT costs; provide ongoing guidance; ensure management engagement and participation; and monitor the project development team's progress.

5 Assessing IT Governance Risks

Risk assessment is an extremely important component of the IT governance process. Identifying and assessing risks can be done by performing a business impact analysis (BIA). The objectives of a BIA are to:

- **Identify IT Resources:** identification of business units, departments, and processes essential to sustain minimum operations.
- **Evaluate Impact and Likelihood of Risks:** categorization of the identified resources by the impact of loss, then by likelihood of that loss occurring.
- **Evaluate Outcomes:** determine the appropriate response, including accepting the risk with no mitigation efforts, avoiding the risk completely by removing the resource, or by implementing some form of mitigation.
- **Implement the Response:** address the areas that are most likely to harm the organization.

A Information Technology (IT) Governance

Question 1   MCQ-14518

Which of the following is responsible for carrying out IT governance policies?

1. Board of directors
2. Executives
3. Middle management
4. End users

Question 2   MCQ-14519

Which of the following represents a company's aspirations and goals?

1. Vision statement
2. Corporate strategy
3. IT strategy
4. Steering committee

1 The Role of IT in Business

The application of information technology (IT) in an organization is the systematic implementation of hardware and software so that data can be transmitted, modified, accessed, and stored.

2 IT Infrastructure

The supporting IT architecture within most companies has multiple, interconnected technological components, with the core infrastructure involving a combination of on-site and outsourced hardware.

2.1 Hardware

The physical components of computers and computer-related accessories are referred to as computer hardware. Hardware includes computer components as well as external peripheral devices.

- **Computer Hardware:** This includes microprocessors, graphics and sound cards, hard drives, random access memory, the power supply, and the motherboard.
- **External Hardware Devices:** These include computer mice, keyboards, speakers, microphones, disk drives, memory devices, network cards, monitors, printers, scanners, and networking equipment.
- **Infrastructure Housing:** This includes advanced security systems to monitor and control access as well as ventilation and climate control.

2.2 Networking Devices

Networking hardware enables connectivity and communication between devices on a computer network.

- **Routers:** Routers manage network traffic by connecting devices to form a network.
- **Switches:** Switches connect and divide devices within a computer network.
- **Gateway:** A gateway is a computer or device that acts as an intermediary between different networks.
- **Servers:** Servers are physical or virtual machines that coordinate the computers, programs, and data.
- **Firewall:** Firewalls are software applications or hardware devices that protect a person's or a company's network traffic.

2.3 Software

Software consists of the applications, procedures, or programs that provide instructions for a computer to execute. Software that is embedded in hardware that instructs the hardware how to operate is known as firmware.

2.4 Networks

A network is a group of computers and other machines that are interconnected electronically using a series of networking devices. Common types of networks include local area networks (LANs) and wide area networks (WANs).

2.5 Mobile Technology

Mobile technology is technology that travels with the user and can allow organizational activities to occur in real time. Mobile technology combines hardware, such as laptops, tablets, hot spots, and mobile phones, with mobile applications and operating systems that allow connectivity to networks.

3 The Role of Management Information Systems

Management information systems (MIS) enable companies to use data as part of their strategic planning process as well as the tactical execution of that strategy. MIS reports provide feedback on daily operations and financial and nonfinancial information to support both internal and external business decisions.

3.1 Accounting Information System (AIS)

The system that accountants and financial managers interact with the most is the AIS. An AIS typically has three subsystems.

- **Transaction Processing System (TPS):** A TPS converts economic events into financial transactions. A TPS typically covers three main transaction cycles: sales cycle, conversion cycle, and expenditure cycle.

- **Financial Reporting System (FRS) or General Ledger System (GLS):** The FRS/GLS aggregates daily financial information from the TPS to enable timely reporting.

- **Management Reporting System (MRS):** An MRS provides internal financial information to solve day-to-day business problems.

An AIS has three main functions:

1. Collect, record, and store data and transactions
2. Transform data into information through compilation and reporting
3. Safeguard and maintain data integrity

3.2 Decision Support System (DSS)

A DSS is an extension of an MIS that provides interactive tools to support day-to-day decision making. It is sometimes called an expert system and may be either an extension of a large management information system or an independent application.

3.3 Executive Information System (EIS)

Executive information systems provide senior executives with immediate and easy access to internal and external information to assist in strategic big-picture decision making. These systems present data in high-level reports and visualizations that allow for decision making to ensure alignment with strategic objectives.

3.4 Customer Relationship Management System (CRM)

CRM is a software that enables organizations to monitor and manage interactions between the organization and its past, current, and potential customers. There are three types of customer relationship management systems:

- **Operational CRM:** The goal of an operational CRM is to generate leads and convert those leads into customers.
- **Analytical CRM:** An analytical CRM is designed to collect and analyze customer information and provide insights to management to aid in decision making.
- **Collaborative or Strategic CRM:** This type of CRM shares customer information across functions such as sales, marketing, service, and support teams.

3.5 Inventory Management

Inventory management systems track item quantities and trigger reordering when quantities fall below a predetermined level.

3.6 Knowledge Management System (KMS)

A KMS refers to any IT system that disseminates knowledge related to the organization.

3.7 Supply Chain Management (SCM)

An integrated supply chain management system connects many activities, such as purchasing, materials handling, production planning and control, logistics and warehousing, inventory control, and product distribution and delivery. SCM systems generally incorporate planning, sourcing, production, and delivery functions.

3.8 Enterprise Resource Planning (ERP)

An ERP system is utilized to support different business functions and allow for the integration of information across departments.

3.9   Enterprise Performance Management (EPM)

EPM systems are software programs designed to help executives make strategic decisions. An EPM enables leaders to plan, budget, and forecast business performances and to consolidate financial results.

EPM systems differ from ERP systems. EPM is more management-process focused, whereas ERP is more focused on operational processes and information technology integration.

3.10 E-Commerce

Electronic commerce platforms facilitate the sale of goods and services using the internet. There are five types of e-commerce:

- **Business-to-Business (B2B):** B2B e-commerce involves the buying and selling of goods and services between business entities.
- **Business-to-Consumer (B2C):** B2C e-commerce allows businesses to sell goods to their customers.
- **Consumer-to-Business (C2B):** In this type of e-commerce, consumers offer their goods or services to a business.
- **Consumer-to-Consumer (C2C):** C2C e-commerce functions as an online marketplace in which individual consumers buy and sell goods with each other.
- **Government E-Commerce:** Government e-commerce can be between the government and any other entity (a consumer or a business).

3.11 Communication

Email is utilized by most companies. Other communication options used are telephone networks, videoconferencing, instant messaging, texting, and social media platforms.

4   IT Outsourcing and Cloud Computing

Some organizations expand beyond their internal IT infrastructure and utilize third-party external service providers. This strategy is known as IT outsourcing and utilizes a variety of IT solutions, including cloud computing, virtualization, and application service providers. Outsourced services include application software, data entry, data storage, data management, disaster recovery, and network management.

4.1   Cloud Computing

Cloud computing is renting storage space, processing power, proprietary software, or a combination of the three, on remote servers of another company rather than buying or building those components. For the customers of cloud computing, the service offers infrastructure elasticity, renting only as much as needed. Customers also benefit because the cloud service provider performs all maintenance and tech support on this hardware.

4.2   IT Outsourcing Advantages

IT outsourcing advantages include lower costs, easy access to IT experts, access to specialized resources, and enhanced focus on the core business.

4.3   IT Outsourcing Disadvantages

The disadvantages of IT outsourcing include less control, uneven quality control, and lack of access to IT personnel.

4.4   IT Outsourcing Risks

IT outsourcing risks include security and privacy risks and vulnerability to attacks.

4.5   System and Organization Controls (SOC)

The System and Organization Controls (SOC) reports are a collection of reports developed by the American Institute of Certified Public Accountants (AICPA) to be issued in connection with the evaluation of "system-level controls" or "entity-level controls" for service-based firms. There are three reports that these types of engagement can produce: a SOC 1® report, a SOC 2® report, and a SOC 3® report.

■ **SOC 1®:** The objective of SOC 1® reports is to provide assurance that the service organization's controls are designed and operating effectively so that the financial statements are not negatively impacted. The use of SOC 1® reports assists in mitigating the inherent risks in outsourcing IT functions. Two types of SOC 1® reports can be provided by service organizations:

- The Type 1 report focuses on the fairness of the presentation of management's description of the service organization's system and the suitability of the design of the controls to achieve the related control objectives included in the description as of a specified date.

- The Type 2 report focuses on the fairness of the presentation of management's description of the service organization's system and the suitability of the design and operating effectiveness of the controls to achieve the related control objectives included in the description through a specified period.

■ **SOC 2®:** A SOC 2® report is for users who need attestation concerning controls as they relate to security, processing integrity, availability, and privacy. These reports are important for vendor management, oversight of a company, risk management, corporate governance, and regulatory oversight. SOC 2® reports also have two types:

- Type 1 is a report of management's explanation or description of a given service company's system as well as the suitability of control design.

- Type 2 is also a report of management's explanation or description of a company's control design and its operating effectiveness of internal controls.

■ **SOC 3®:** SOC 3® reports are also for users who need attestation concerning controls as they relate to security, processing integrity, availability, and privacy. However, this report is for companies that do not have the knowledge required to make an effective use of a SOC 2® report.

Question 1   MCQ-14520

Which of the following is a disadvantage of outsourcing?

1. Access to specialized resources
2. Enhanced focus on the core business
3. Less control
4. Reduced costs

Question 2   MCQ-14521

A large retail company employs an e-commerce system through which customers can buy directly from the company via the company's website. What business model is the company using?

1. Business-to-business (B2B)
2. Business-to-consumer (B2C)
3. Consumer-to-business (C2B)
4. Consumer-to-consumer (C2C)

1 The Evolving Role of Big Data in the Decision-Making Process

In today's world, the type and volume of data being created have increased at unprecedented rates. To leverage the power of this data, companies must capture it, store it, protect, and eventually dispose of it, if appropriate.

1.1 Defining Data

Data can be defined as a fact, occurrence, instance, or other measurable observation. Data can be numerical digits, alphanumeric text, images, video, or audio recordings.

1.2 Defining Big Data

Big Data refers to the corporate accumulation of massive amounts of data that can be used for analysis (data analytics).

1.3 Dimensions of Big Data

There are five dimensions of Big Data, often referred to as the Five Vs of Big Data:

- **Volume:** Volume represents the quantity or amount of data points.
- **Velocity:** Velocity refers to the speed of data accumulation or data processing.
- **Variety:** Variety refers to the range of data types being processed or analyzed. Three general categories of data are structured data, unstructured data, or semi-structured data.
- **Veracity:** Veracity represents the reliability, quality, or integrity of the data.
- **Value:** Value refers to the insights Big Data can yield.

1.4 Big Data Governance

Big Data comes with challenges, such as ethical and legal concerns pertaining to the organization itself, employees, customers, and stakeholders. An IT governance program should provide guidance on how sensitive data should be captured, maintained, and disposed of during its life cycle.

- **Big Data Confidentiality:** Confidential information must be safeguarded to protect it from unauthorized access and exploitation.
- **Big Data Privacy:** Customer and patient information must also be safeguarded from unauthorized access to meet consumer privacy expectations as well as regulatory requirements.

- **Big Data Ethics:** Organizations should make sure authorized personnel are granted the minimum level of access to the data necessary to perform their job functions. This includes assigning rights that limit users' ability to create, read, edit, and delete data based on role and job function.

- **Governance Responsibility:** An organization's governance program should be led by a designated individual. Management of the program should involve all aspects of an organization that captures, maintains, stores, and uses data of any kind.

2 Data Management

Data management is key for every organization. Ensuring that the data is maintained and stored appropriately is vital to the decision-making process.

2.1   Storing Data in Relational Databases

- One of the most efficient and effective methods for data storage is a relational database. Relational databases allow data stored in different tables to be linked through relationships using key fields.

- Relational databases key concepts include tables, attributes (columns), records (rows), fields, data types, and database keys.

- A data dictionary, also referred to as metadata, provides information about the data in a database. A data dictionary typically lists each attribute as well as features and limitations of that attribute. Features include the data type, field size of length, and whether the data is a primary, foreign, or non-key attribute.

- Database views are of two broad types: logical and physical.

  - **Logical Database View:** The logical view is how the data appears to a user. It is what the user sees.

  - **Physical Database View:** The physical view pertains to how the data is actually stored within the database.

- Extracting data can be done with query tools. Once a query is designed and executed, the results of the query can be visually displayed in a database report. End users utilize the reports to assist with data analysis and decision making.

3 Extract, Transform, and Load

It is important to understand the extract, transform, and load process (ETL). This is the process in which data is captured from its source and transferred to an organization's custody so that it can be further analyzed.

3.1 Data Extraction

Data extraction can be an automated process, semiautomated process, or manual extraction. The source and means of accessing the data must be determined in the initial ETL setup phase. This will dictate the tools needed for designing the extraction process.

3.2 Transforming the Data

One of the most time-consuming steps in the ETL process is the transformation step because it entails taking the often-unstructured data, cleaning it, and validating it to ensure that it is accurate and ready for analysis.

3.3 Loading the Data

The final step of the ETL process is to load the data into a software program for analysis or into a data storage location.

- **Storing Data:** Data can be stored in a variety of locations/repositories, including an operational data store, a data warehouse, a data mart, or a data lake.

- **Data Storage Requirements:** Special considerations and constraints apply to relational databases. Primary keys must be utilized for a database to establish and maintain entity integrity. In a relational database, a change to a primary key in one table must also cause a change to any related foreign key in a linked table. This maintains the referential integrity of the database.

- **Data Storage Attributes:** The purpose of a data repository must be defined to help users understand a repository's relevance. Defining which attributes are included will outline the universe of data points housed within a repository. The relationships among data must be maintained to ensure validity, completeness, and accuracy.

- **Types of Loading:** Data loading can take several forms, including initial (full) loading, incremental loading, and full refresh loading.

4 Data Analytics

Data analytics is the process of taking raw data, identifying trends, and then transforming that knowledge into insights that can help solve complex business problems. There are four key applications in data analytics.

4.1 Descriptive Analytics

Descriptive analytics indicate what happened. This form of analytics summarizes the activity that has occurred within a given attribute or attributes.

4.2 Diagnostic Analytics

Diagnostic analytics reveal why an event happened. This goes a step beyond descriptive analytics and attempts to uncover correlations, patterns, and relationships within a data set to explain why an event or result occurred.

4.3   Predictive Analytics

Predictive analytics help forecast future data points by transforming insight into foresight, and project what will happen based on historical data. Common predictive analytic techniques include regression analysis, classification analysis, and decision trees.

4.4   Prescriptive Analytics

Prescriptive analytics reveal how to achieve a desired event by "prescribing" what the next course of action should be in order to reach that outcome. Prescriptive analytics take the probability learned from predictive analytics and turn that into recommendations and optimal paths with a high likelihood of favorable outcomes. Common prescriptive analytic techniques include artificial intelligence and scenario modeling.

Data analytics can be used in many aspects of the decision-making process: customer and marketing analytics, managerial and operational analytics, risk and compliance analytics, financial analytics, audit analytics, and tax analytics.

5 Data Visualizations

It is important to select the right communication technique when interpreting insights from Big Data analysis. Turning complex data sets into easily read and understood visualizations make the decision process more accessible, efficient, and effective for decision makers.

5.1   Types of Data

The type of data being presented can determine the choice of data visualization utilized.

- **Qualitative Data:** Qualitative data is nonnumerical and categorical in nature. Nominal qualitative data is the simplest form and cannot be ordered or ranked. Ordinal qualitative data is categorical and not quantitative, but it can be ranked in a meaningful way, such as from cold to hot.

- **Quantitative Data:** Quantitative data is numerical in nature. Quantitative data may be discrete or continuous. Discrete values are whole numbers and can only have certain values. Continuous data can take on any value (including decimal values) within a given (finite or infinite) range.

5.2 Types of Data Visualizations

There are many different visualization types and techniques.

- Line charts
- Column charts
- Stacked column charts
- Scatter plots
- Boxplots
- Dot plots
- Geographic maps
- Symbol maps
- Pie charts
- Pyramid
- Flowcharts
- Waterfall charts
- Directional charts

5.3 Design Considerations for Data Visualizations

- **Scale Appropriately:** The scaling of the axes should not be misleading. Typically, numeric value scaling should start at zero.
- **Use Legends Appropriately:** If there are more than four or five colors, avoid using a legend.
- **Avoid Bias:** Do not present data in such a way that would direct the reader toward a specific conclusion.
- **Use Consistent Time Periods:** Do not compare results from a longer period with those from a shorter period.
- **Use of Color:** Use colors that can be easily seen and follow cultural norms.
- **Use Clear and Easy-to-Read Titles and Labels:** Labels should be used sparingly or only when accuracy is necessary.

C Data Management and Analytics

Question 1 — MCQ-14522

An organization has decided to analyze social media postings concerning the industry in which it operates. The resulting data includes text, numbers, images, and videos. Which Big Data dimension best describes this data?

1. Volume
2. Velocity
3. Veracity
4. Variety

Question 2 — MCQ-14523

If an organization is analyzing sales by looking at the average sales by region, which type of data analytics process is it implementing?

1. Predictive analytics
2. Diagnostic analytics
3. Prescriptive analytics
4. Descriptive analytics

System Development and Change Management

1 Evolving the IT Infrastructure

As information technology (IT) equipment reaches the end of its useful life and as technology advances, organizations update their IT infrastructure over time to keep pace with these shifts or to be early adopters. Organizations can update existing software and hardware, acquire or change to new hardware and software, or develop infrastructure. All of these approaches can be effective and come with potential risks that must be managed.

2 Change Management Overview

Change management is used to describe policies, procedures, and resources employed to govern change in an organization. The scope of change can range from something as routine as implementing a new marketing technique to an initiative more complex and infrequent as overhauling an organization's IT infrastructure. With any change, potential risks need to be mitigated to minimize disruption to core business functions and operations.

A robust change management process is a key component for successfully ensuring that an organization can keep up with changing needs without losing the ability to operate or achieve its strategic objectives.

3 Change Management Risks

A key component of change management is to identify the potential risks that could occur as a result of the change. These risks are present in all steps of change from acquisition to implementation and can affect existing systems, processes, and employees.

3.1 Selection and Acquisition Risks

- **Lack of Expertise:** When purchasing software, there is the risk that the purchasing agent does not have the expertise or organizational perspective to purchase software that meets the needs of the organization.

- **Lack of Formal Selection and Acquisition Process:** This is the risk that an organization either does not have, or does not follow, a formal selection and acquisition process. This could result in overspending, inappropriate related party transactions or kickbacks, or software that does not align with the IT governance strategy.

- **Software/Hardware Vulnerability and Incompatibility:** There is the risk that proper safeguards and security features do not exist. There is also the risk that newly acquired hardware and software are incompatible with existing resources that will remain in production.

3.2   Integration Risks

- **User Resistance:** There is a risk that employees do not adapt to change, ignore training, and ultimately do not follow through with change appropriately.

- **Lack of Management Support:** If management does not provide both resources and adequate support, employee resistance is magnified.

- **Lack of Stakeholder Support:** Stakeholders, including employees, suppliers, and customers, may have an adverse reaction or disposition toward change.

- **Resource Concerns:** Appropriate resources may not be made available for the change, which may lead to ineffective implementation.

- **Business Disruptions:** Change could cause significant disruptions to core functions and could have long-term negative consequences on the organization.

- **Lack of System Integration:** Organizations operate many different systems, some of which may not effectively adapt or integrate with more modern systems.

3.3   Outsourcing Risks

Outsourcing change management saves costs but comes with risks.

- **Lack of Organizational Knowledge:** Disruptions could occur if a third party does not comprehend the organization's business model.

- **Uncertainty of the Third Party's Knowledge and Management:** There is a risk that the external party has ineffective or weak management, inexperienced or underqualified staff, or a lack of technology expertise.

- **Lack of Security:** There is a risk that an external organization does not have sufficient or effective safeguards to make sure that client, customer, employee, or operational information is kept secure.

4 Change Management Controls

4.1 Change Management and New Systems Controls

Once all risks in the change management process have been identified, controls are designed to minimize the possibility that risks will cause business disruptions or negatively impact IT systems. Change management controls include the following:

- Policies and procedures
- Emergency change policies
- Standardized change requests
- Impact assessment
- Authorization
- Separation of duties
- Conversion controls
- Reversion access
- Pre-implementation testing
- Post-implementation testing
- Ongoing monitoring

4.2 Outsourcing Controls

One of the drawbacks to outsourcing change management and IT functions is a lack of control over the process. It is very important to monitor the controls and address any issues or problems in a timely fashion. Examples of outsourcing controls include the following:

- Outsourcing policies and procedures
- System and organization controls (SOC) reports
- Utilization of key performance indicators (KPIs)

5 Managing Risks of Systems Development

Organizations may acquire a new system or choose to develop a new system in-house. Both processes have their own risks and concerns but still follow the general systems development life cycle.

5.1   Systems Development Life Cycle

The systems development life cycle (SDLC) provides a model for organizations to create, modify, or acquire information systems to meet the needs of organizations and their users. The SDLC guides an organization through seven key steps:

1. **Plan:** Evaluate the need for a new or improved information system.
2. **Analyze:** Gather information from all vital stakeholders.
3. **Design:** Start designing the system to meet agreed-upon user needs.
4. **Develop:** Execute the technical implementation plan created in prior phases.
5. **Test:** Check the system for adherence to the business requirements.
6. **Deploy:** Document an implementation strategy to deliver the system to end users.
7. **Maintain:** Make ongoing adjustments and improvements to keep the system operating at an optimal level.

5.2   Systems Development and New Systems Risks

An organization faces many risks in the systems development life cycle. These risks can cause delays, inefficiencies, and wasted resources.

- **Resource Risk:** This is the risk that allocation of resources related to finance, labor, or time is insufficient.
- **Scheduling Risk:** If schedules are not met, if they do not factor in uncertainties, or if a scope expansion happens, the entire project will be delayed.
- **Technical Risk:** This is the risk that the development team does not have the required technical knowledge or that the technical design and functionality do not align with user needs.
- **Project Management Risk:** This is the risk that the project management team does not have clearly defined leadership, team member roles, responsibilities, and project goals.
- **User Resistance Risk:** This is the risk that employees will not accept the new system.

6 Managing Risks of Legacy Systems

Maintaining legacy systems is common at many organizations due to many factors, such as comfort with existing systems and unwillingness to pay for upgrades.

6.1   Reasons for Persistence of Legacy Systems

- **Costs:** The cost to purchase or develop a new system can be extremely high.
- **Time:** Implementing a new system means allocation of employee time.
- **User Resistance:** Users may be comfortable with the old system and resistant to change.
- **Features and Customization:** Existing systems may have features that are difficult to replicate.
- **Risk of Information Loss:** Transferring data to a new system risks having data and information corrupted or lost.

6.2   Risks of Legacy Systems

- **Security Vulnerability:** Legacy systems may be vulnerable regarding security, including hacking and cyberattacks.
- **Lack of Vendor Support:** Eventually support for legacy systems will end.
- **Compatibility Issues:** Legacy systems may be incompatible with modern systems.
- **Lack of Efficiency and Effectiveness:** Legacy systems may not be able to compare with the speed or reliability of a modern system.

6.3   Mitigating Risks of Legacy Systems

- **Isolate the System:** Isolating a risk legacy system from other systems in a separate physical or virtual environment can help limit the potential in the event someone gains unauthorized access.
- **Hardening:** This involves turning off any unnecessary features of the legacy system to reduce potential exposure.
- **Virtual Patches:** If no security patches are available for legacy software or hardware, a virtual patch could be applied at the network level before it reaches the legacy system.
- **Monitoring:** Frequent review and monitoring of legacy system logs and changes help to detect any unusual system activity.

7 Information System and Change Management Testing Strategies

An ongoing testing plan for information technology is necessary to detect problems or functional issues.

7.1 Purpose of Testing

Testing software that was developed in-house determines whether the software is operating as expected; discovers errors, defects, and gaps in the software; and verifies that the end product meets the business and user requirements.

7.2 Software Testing Process

The software testing process generally follows these six steps:

1. Establish a testing plan including roles, responsibilities, and a time line.
2. Identify and prioritize the key areas of the software to test.
3. Determine which type of test to run and specify the test objectives.
4. Execute the tests.
5. Log the results and identify defects.
6. Report the findings and fix the defects in a timely manner.

7.3 Guidelines for Successful Testing

The following steps represent best practices for testing:

- Develop a test plan that identifies major bugs early in the development process.
- Build robust software that allows for automated testing.
- Conduct formal technical reviews to assess the test strategy and test cases.
- Develop a continuous test approach over the life cycle of the software.

7.4 Type of Tests

The complex nature of systems development requires a variety of systems testing.

- **Unit Tests:** Unit tests are used to validate the smallest components of the system.
- **Integration Tests:** Integration testing determines if the units function together as designed.
- **Systems Tests:** Systems tests evaluate the system as a whole and take on many forms.
  - Functional tests focus on testing the functions performed by the system.
  - Black-box testing focuses on testing the system as an end user would validate outcomes.

- White-box testing focuses on code and design improvement as opposed to testing functionality.

- Exploratory tests are utilized for the less-common or exception-based situations.

- Performance testing is designed to test the run-time performance of software.

- Recovery tests check the system's ability to recover from failures.

- Security testing verifies that authorized access levels function properly.

- Regression tests rerun test cases within the entire application.

- Stress testing checks the program to see how well it deals with abnormal resource demands.

- Sanity testing exercises the logical reasoning and behavior of the software.

- **Acceptance Tests:** An acceptance test determines whether the software works correctly.

  - **Alpha Test:** The initial version of the completed software is tested by the customer under the supervision of the developer at the developer's site.

  - **Beta Test:** A later version of the complete software is tested at the customer's own site without the developer being present.

7.5   Change Management Testing

Testing of the change management process and controls generally occur both within the organization (compliance, management review, and internal audit) and outside the organization (regulators and external auditors).

Question 1   MCQ-14524

In which step of the systems development process does an organization evaluate the need for a new or improved information system?

1. Analyze
2. Design
3. Develop
4. Plan

Question 2   MCQ-14525

Which type of test checks the system to see how well it deals with abnormal resource demands?

1. Sanity test
2. Stress test
3. Regression test
4. Security test

---

1 Understanding IT Risks

As organizations integrate more technology into their operations, new and greater risks materialize. The security life cycle is the process for identifying and addressing risks.

1. **Identify:** Identify and document risks associated with technology assets.
2. **Assess:** Determine the likelihood of the risk and the level of impact.
3. **Protect:** Develop security policies and mitigation strategies.
4. **Monitor:** Continually monitor activities and acquisitions for new risks.

2 Identifying IT Risks

2.1 Technology Risk

Technology risk is the risk of disruption to business due to information technology activity.

- **Security Risk:** The risk associated with unauthorized access or use of an organization's information technology.
- **Availability Risk:** The risk that an organization is not able to access and utilize its information technology.
- **Operational Risk:** The risk that an organization is unable to operate effectively or efficiently due to IT issues.
- **Financial Risk:** The risk of losing financial resources as a result of misuse.
- **Compliance Risk:** The risk of not meeting the requirements of regulatory bodies.
- **Strategic Risk:** The risk of misalignment of business and IT strategies.

2.2 Types of IT Threats

- Natural and political disasters
- Errors in software and equipment malfunctions
- Accidental actions
- Intentional actions

2.3   Risk Management

To successfully manage risk, organizations must meet the following three objectives:

1. Integrate the management of IT risk into the overall risk management of the enterprise.

2. Make well-informed decisions about the nature and extent of the risk, the risk appetite, and the risk tolerance of the enterprise.

3. Develop a response to the risk.

2.4   IT Risk Mitigation Strategies and Roles

IT risks cannot be mitigated through software and hardware-based controls alone. Management must determine what the overall risk appetite is for the organization and develop a security strategy that includes policies and procedures to align that risk appetite with information systems and information technology.

- **Confidentiality, Integrity, and Availability Triangle:** These risks are addressed with access and authorization controls, segregation of duties, and data processing controls.

- **Management's Risk Philosophy:** Risk appetite must be determined to build appropriate information security policies and procedures.

- **Establishing a Security Policy:** A security policy defines how an organization plans to protect its IT infrastructure and resources.

- **Security Policy Goals:** The goal of a good security policy is to protect the IT infrastructure and information.

- **Security Communication:** The security policy should be communicated to everyone within an organization.

3   The Role and Categorization of IT Controls

IT controls fall into two broad categories: general IT controls and application IT controls. Their functions are to prevent, detect, or correct issues and deficiencies.

3.1   Categories of IT Controls

- **General IT Controls (GITCs):** General controls are designed to ensure that an organization's control environment is stable and well-managed.

- **Application Controls:** Application controls are typically built into business processes that use computer applications. Application controls should ensure that transactions and data processed is accurate, complete, valid, and authorized.

- **Software/Hardware Vulnerability and Incompatibility:** There is the risk that proper safeguards and security features that are needed do not exist. There is also the risk that newly acquired hardware and software are incompatible with existing resources that will remain in production.

3.2 Nature of IT Controls

■ **Manual Controls:** A control performed by a person without making direct use of automated systems.

■ **Automated Controls:** A control performed by an automated system, without interference of a person.

■ **IT-Dependent Manual Controls:** A control that has components of both manual and automated controls.

3.3 Function of IT Controls

■ **Preventive Controls:** The function of preventive controls is to take precautions to prevent problems in the future.

■ **Detective Controls:** The function of detective controls is to find issues or deficiencies not averted by preventive controls.

■ **Corrective Controls:** Corrective controls are designed to identify, repair, restore, and recover from issues that cause damage to a system or process.

4 System Access and Segregation of Duties

4.1 Logical Access Controls

Logical access controls utilize software and protocols to monitor and control access to information and an organization's IT infrastructure.

■ **Use Access Controls:** These controls identify user access and track user activity.

■ **Authentication Controls:** These controls verify the unique identity of individuals accessing the system.

- **Passwords:** A combination of characters known only to the user.
- **Personal Identification Numbers (PINs):** Numeric code that acts as an identifier.
- **Biometrics:** Physical characteristics such as an iris scan, fingerprint, or voice recognition.
- **Physical Tokens:** A physical device that has an embedded chip or bar code that can be scanned.
- **Push Notifications:** Verification on a separate device owned by the user, such as a cell phone.
- **Multifactor Authentication:** A technique that requires more than one form of authentication.

■ **Managing Passwords:** Passwords protect access to secure systems and may include the following characteristics:

- **Password Requirement:** Every account must have a password.
- **Password Length:** Longer passwords are more effective.

- **Password Complexity:** Strong passwords are a combination of uppercase, lowercase, numeric, and ASCII characters.
- **Password Age:** Passwords should be changed frequently to be effective.
- **Password Reuse:** Passwords should not be reused.

- **Access Control Lists:** A list of users and applications with rights granted (create or write access; read-only access, update access; and delete permission).
- **Personnel Changes:** Controls implemented when individuals are onboarded, promoted, or discharged.
- **Network Security:** A firewall prevents unauthorized access to an organization's network.
- **Vulnerability Controls:** Controls to ensure proper authorization and usage.
    - **Hardening:** Turning off features or functions that are not needed during operations.
    - **Patch Management:** Addressing vulnerabilities with patches (fixes) before they are exploited.
    - **Anti-Malware Programs:** Software to monitor and identify threats.
- **Data Encryption:** Use of a password or a digital key to scramble a readable message into an unreadable message. The intended recipient uses another digital key to decrypt the ciphered message.
- **Digital Certificates:** Electronic documents that are digitally signed by a trusted party.
- **Digital Signatures vs. E-Signatures:** Digital signatures use asymmetric encryption to create legally binding electronic documents. E-signature is a cursive-style imprint of an individual's name that is applied to an electronic document.

4.2 Physical Controls

Physical controls monitor and control the workplace environment and computing facilities. They include:

- Locked doors requiring keys, access cards, pass codes, or biometric scanners.
- Secure pass-throughs called mantraps.
- Physical obstructions such as fencing and barricades.
- Security systems connected to local law enforcement.
- Monitoring safeguards such as security guards and cameras.

4.3 Segregation of Duties

Segregation of duties reduces opportunities for anyone to both perpetrate and conceal errors or fraud in the normal course of one's duties.

- **System Analysts vs. Computer Programmers:** System analysts design an information system to meet user needs, whereas computer programmers use that design to create an information system by writing computer programs. If the same person is responsible for hardware and software, that person could easily bypass security systems and steal organizational information or assets.

- **Security Administrators vs. Computer Operators and Computer Programmers:** Security administrators are responsible for assigning and restricting access to systems, applications, or databases to the appropriate personnel. If the security administrator were also a programmer for that system, that individual could gain access to unauthorized areas or give access to another person.

5 Risks and Controls of Critical, Confidential, and Private Information

Critical, confidential, and private information all need to be safeguarded to ensure that the organization, its employees, its customers, and other stakeholders are protected appropriately.

- Critical information is any information that is vital for the organization to perform its essential functions and achieve its strategic objectives.

- Confidentiality refers to the efforts to keep information within or about the organization from being misused or accessed without authorization.

- Privacy involves the rights of employees and customers to keep their personal information safe.

- Organizations must ensure that they have an incident program in place to address unauthorized access or the theft or misuse of critical, confidential, or private data.

E IT Risks and Responses

6 System Availability and Business Resiliency

- System availability risks pertain to system availability and include failure of IT infrastructure, insufficient capacity and resources, and lack of business resiliency.

- Business resiliency is the integration of system availability controls, crisis management, disaster recovery plans, and business continuity plans.

- System availability controls are activities to prevent system disruptions and loss of information.

- Crisis management plans define roles, responsibilities, and procedures to deal with crisis situations.

- Disaster recovery plans are plans for restoring and continuing the information technology function in the event of a disaster. An organization has three main options for maintaining IT operations: cold site, hot site, and warm site.

- Business continuity plans focus on keeping the business operational during a disaster.

- Business resiliency services are offered by companies with specialized knowledge and resources and include disaster recovery as a service, backup as a service, and business continuity as a service.

Question 1   MCQ-14526

Which of the following is an example of a physical control?

   1. Authentication controls
   2. Data encryption
   3. Digital certificates
   4. Security systems connected to local law enforcement

Question 2   MCQ-14527

What IT risk is defined as the risk of not meeting the requirements of regulatory bodies?

   1. Availability risk
   2. Compliance risk
   3. Financial risk
   4. Strategic risk

V | Operations Management

A Performance Management

B Cost Accounting

C Process Management

D Budgeting and Analysis

E Forecasting and Projection

1 Financial and Nonfinancial Performance Measures

1.1 Financial Measures

The following are used as a financial measure of performance:

- Profit is the amount of income generated after expenses.

- Return on investment is the income generated based on a given investment (e.g., total assets employed, stockholders' equity).

- Variance analysis compares actual performance to expected performance.

- Balance scorecard is a framework used to convert an entity's strategic objectives into a set of performance measures.

1.2 Nonfinancial Measures

1.2.1 External Benchmarks

External benchmarks/productivity measures include:

- Total factor productivity ratios (TFPs) reflect the quantity of all output produced relative to the costs of all inputs used.

- Partial productivity ratios (PPRs) reflect the quantity of output produced relative to the quantity of individual inputs used.

1.2.2 Internal Benchmarks

Internal benchmarks/techniques for analyzing problems:

- A control chart is a graphical tool used to plot a comparison of actual results by batch to an acceptable range to determine improvement or deterioration of quality conformance.

- A Pareto diagram is used to plot the frequency of defects from the highest to lowest frequency.

- Cause-and-effect (fishbone) diagrams are used to identify recurring and costly defects and then break down the problems that led to the individual defects.

1.3 Characteristics of Effective Performance Measures

Effective performance measures promote the achievement of goals. Typically, the characteristics of those measures:

- relate to the goals of the organization;

- balance long- and short-term issues;

- reflect management of key activities, sometimes referred to as critical success factors in the balanced scorecard;

- are under the control or influence of the employee;

- are understood by the employee;

- are used to both evaluate and reward the employee or otherwise constructively influence behavior;

- are objective and easily measured; and

- are used consistently.

Question 1   MCQ-09699

The Long Haul Trucking Company is developing metrics for its drivers. The company computes variable costs of each load based upon miles driven and allocates fixed costs based upon time consumed. Load costing standards consider safe driving speeds and Department of Transportation regulations on hours of service (the amount of time the driver can be on duty or drive). The most effective metric for driver performance would likely be:

1. Contribution per mile driven.

2. Gross margin per mile driven.

3. Achievement of delivered loads in allowed times.

4. Percentage increase in delivered loads below standard.

---

2 ROI and ROA

2.1 ROI

- Return on investment (ROI) provides for the assessment of a company's percentage return relative to its capital investment risk.

- ROI is calculated as follows:

> ROI = Net income / Average invested capital
>
> OR
>
> ROI = Profit margin × Investment turnover

2.2 ROA

- Return on assets (ROA) is similar to ROI, except that ROA uses average total assets in the denominator rather than invested capital.

- ROA is calculated as follows:

$$\text{Return on assets} = \frac{\text{Net income}}{\text{Average total assets}}$$

Question 2   MCQ-09208

The following information pertains to Quest Co.'s Gold Division for Year 4:

Sales	$311,000
Variable cost	250,000
Traceable fixed costs	50,000
Average invested capital	40,000
Imputed interest rate	10%

Quest's return on investment was:

1. 10%
2. 13.33%
3. 27.5%
4. 30%

3 ROE and DuPont Ratios

3.1 ROE

A measure of profitability, return on equity (ROE) is the amount of net income returned as a percentage of shareholder's equity.

$$\text{ROE} = \frac{\text{Net income}}{\text{Average total equity}}$$

3.2 DuPont Ratio

The DuPont ratio is a means for breaking down ROE into three components:

$$\text{DuPont ROE} = \text{Net profit margin} \times \text{Asset turnover} \times \text{Financial leverage}$$

$$= \frac{\text{Net income}}{\text{Sales}} \times \frac{\text{Sales}}{\text{Average total assets}} \times \frac{\text{Average total assets}}{\text{Average total equity}}$$

3.3 Extended DuPont Ratio

The extended DuPont ratio breaks down ROE into five components:

$$\text{Extended DuPont ROE} = \text{Tax burden} \times \text{Interest burden} \times \text{Operating income margin} \times \text{Asset turnover} \times \text{Financial leverage}$$

$$= \frac{\text{Net income}}{\text{Pretax income}} \times \frac{\text{Pretax income}}{\text{EBIT}} \times \frac{\text{EBIT}}{\text{Sales}} \times \frac{\text{Sales}}{\text{Average total assets}} \times \frac{\text{Average total assets}}{\text{Average total equity}}$$

4 Residual Income and Economic Value Added

4.1 Residual Income

■ The formula for residual income is as follows:

$$\text{Residual income} = \text{Net income (from the income statement)} - \text{Required return}$$

Where:

$$\text{Required return} = \text{Net book value (Equity)} \times \text{Hurdle rate}$$

- The hurdle rate used is the cost of equity, which can be established by management or calculated using any of the traditional methods (CAPM, DCF, BYRP).

4.2   Economic Value Added

- The formula for Economic Value Added™ (EVA™) is as follows:

> Economic value added = Net operating profit after taxes − Required return

Where:

> Required return = Investment × Cost of capital

- The cost of capital used is typically the weighted average cost of capital (WACC).

Question 3   MCQ-09216

Following is information relating to Kew Co.'s Vale Division for Year 4:

Sales	$500,000
Variable cost	300,000
Traceable fixed costs	50,000
Average invested capital	100,000
Imputed interest rate	6%

Vale's residual income was:

1. $144,000
2. $150,000
3. $156,000
4. $200,000

---

1 Cost Objects

Cost objects (objectives) are resources or activities that serve as the basis for management decisions.

1.1 Product Costs

- Product costs comprise all costs related to the manufacturing of a product.
- Components of product costs include direct material, direct labor, and manufacturing overhead applied.
- Product costs are inventoriable and traceable (e.g., work in process inventory, finished goods inventory, and cost of goods sold).

1.2 Period Costs

Period costs (e.g., selling, general and administrative expenses) are expensed in the period in which they are incurred and are not inventoriable.

1.3 Manufacturing Costs

- Manufacturing costs (e.g., direct materials, direct labor, and manufacturing overhead) include all costs associated with the manufacturing of a product.
- Manufacturing costs include both direct and indirect costs.

1.4 Nonmanufacturing Costs

- Nonmanufacturing costs are costs that do not relate to the manufacturing of a product, such as advertising costs and salaries of sales personnel.
- Nonmanufacturing costs are expensed in the period incurred.

2 Tracing Costs to Cost Objects

2.1 Direct Costs

- A direct cost can be easily traced to the cost pool or cost object.
- Direct costs include direct raw materials and direct labor.

2.2   Indirect Costs

- An indirect cost is not easily traced to the cost pool or cost object.

- Also known as manufacturing overhead, indirect costs include indirect materials, indirect labor, and other indirect costs (e.g., machine maintenance costs).

- Indirect costs are allocated to cost pools/objects using cost drivers that have a significant relationship to the incurrence of these costs.

3 Cost Behavior

3.1   Variable Costs

- A variable cost varies in total as production volume increases or decreases, but remains constant on a per unit basis.

- Direct materials and direct labor are variable costs.

3.2   Fixed Costs

- A fixed cost remains constant in total, regardless if the production volume increases or decreases, but varies per unit.

- Depreciation would be classified as a fixed cost.

- Over a long-run time horizon, any cost can be considered variable.

3.3   Semi-variable Costs (Mixed Costs)

Semi-variable costs are costs that contain both fixed and variable components (e.g., water utilities, where there is a fixed monthly charge plus a variable rate per gallon used).

3.4   Relevant Range

- The relevant range is the (graphical) range for which the assumptions of a cost driver are valid.

- Any cost driver activity that is outside the relevant range cannot be used to allocate costs to objects.

Question 1 MCQ-09147

Applewhite Corporation, a manufacturing company, is analyzing its cost structure in a project to achieve some cost savings. Which of the following statements is/are correct?

I. The cost of the raw materials in Applewhite's products is considered a variable cost.

II. The cost of the depreciation of Applewhite's factory machinery is considered a variable cost because Applewhite uses an accelerated depreciation method for both book and income tax purposes.

III. The cost of electricity for Applewhite's manufacturing facility is considered a fixed cost, even if the cost of the electricity has both variable and fixed components.

1. I, II, and III are correct.
2. I only is correct.
3. II and III only are correct.
4. None of the listed choices is correct.

4 Cost Accumulation Systems

Cost accumulation systems are used to assign costs to products. Use job order costing when the cost object is a custom order (a batch of business cards). Use process costing when the cost object is a mass-produced homogeneous product (canned vegetables).

5 Cost of Goods Manufactured and Sold

5.1 Cost of Goods Manufactured

The cost of goods manufactured statement accounts for the manufacturing costs of the products completed during the period. Cost of goods manufactured is used as part of the cost of goods sold computation.

Beginning WIP		XXX
Direct materials used	XXX	
Direct labor	XXX	
Factory overhead *applied**	<u>XXX</u>	
Total manufacturing costs		<u>XXX</u>
Manufacturing costs available		XXX
Less: Ending WIP		<u>\<XXX\></u>
Cost of goods manufactured		<u>XXX</u>

* Factory overhead is applied based on a predetermined rate. In traditional costing, estimated costs are divided by a common divisor, such as direct labor hours, direct labor costs, or machine hours. The formula for the traditional overhead application method is as follows:

$$\text{Predetermined OH rate} \ = \ \frac{\text{Estimated total overhead costs}}{\text{Estimated total direct labor hours or other divisors}}$$

5.2   Cost of Goods Sold

Cost of goods sold is the amount matched against sales revenue as part of income determination.

Beginning finished goods inventory	XXX
Cost of goods manufactured	<u>XXX</u>
= Cost of goods available for sale	XXX
Less: Ending finished goods inventory	<u>\<XXX\></u>
Cost of goods sold	<u>XXX</u>

If overhead applied is greater than the total actual overhead costs incurred, we say overhead is overapplied. If the applied overhead is less than the actual, we have underapplied overhead. Overapplied overhead is closed to cost of goods sold as a credit to the expense. Underapplied overhead is closed to cost of goods sold as a debit to the expense.

Question 2

Culpepper Corporation had the following inventories at the beginning and end of the month of January:

	January 1	January 31
Finished goods	$125,000	$117,000
Work-in-process	235,000	251,000
Direct materials	134,000	124,000

The following additional manufacturing data was available for the month of January:

Direct materials purchased	$189,000
Purchase returns and allowances	1,000
Transportation in	3,000
Direct labor	400,000
Actual factory overhead	175,000

Culpepper Corporation applies factory overhead at a rate of 40 percent of direct labor cost, and any overapplied or underapplied factory overhead is deferred until the end of the year. Culpepper's balance in its factory overhead control account at the end of January was:

1. $15,000 overapplied.
2. $15,000 underapplied.
3. $5,000 underapplied.
4. $5,000 overapplied.

6 Job Order Costing

Job order costing is a cost accumulation or product costing method that involves unique or easily identifiable units. This method is used when manufacturing custom products such as customized cars, boats and houses.

- Costs are allocated to a specific job as it moves through the manufacturing process.

- Job cost records or job orders accumulate all costs for a specific job with data obtained from material requisitions and labor time cards.

- Once the job is complete, the total cost is readily available on the job cost record.

7 Process Costing

Process costing accumulates costs by department or process. Two methods are used: FIFO and weighted average. Generally, equivalent units and cost per equivalent unit must be calculated. Unit and cost flow assumptions are specific to each method.

7.1 Application

Process costing is used in those instances in which homogenous units of output are produced and average costing is appropriate. Applications include fuel refining, chemical processing, and paper production.

Transfers in from other departments are always considered 100 percent complete. The transfer in costs of direct material from a previous department are treated as direct materials (DM), even though they are called "transfer in" costs or "previous department" costs.

Direct material added at the beginning of or during a second or later process may either be 100 percent complete or "partially complete," depending on how much work has been done on that component of the process.

Any material added at the (very) end of a process will not be in work in process inventory at the month end.

7.2 Equivalent Units

An equivalent unit of direct material, direct labor, or conversion costs is equal to the amount of direct material, direct labor, or conversion costs necessary to complete one unit of production. Equivalent units of production may be computed using either first-in first-out (FIFO) or weighted average assumptions. The FIFO approach specifically accounts for work to be completed during a period, while the weighted average approach accounts for work completed during the period as well as the work performed last period on this period's beginning inventory.

7.2.1 FIFO (Three Steps)

Beginning WIP × % to be completed	XXX
Units completed—Beginning WIP	XXX
Ending WIP × % completed	XXX
Equivalent units	XXX

7.2.2   Weighted Average (Two Steps)

Units completed	XXX
Ending WIP × % completed	XXX
Equivalent units	XXX

7.3   Cost per Equivalent Units

Cost per equivalent unit is computed by dividing total costs by equivalent units. FIFO anticipates using only current period costs, while the weighted average approach uses both costs of beginning inventory and current period costs as follows:

7.3.1   FIFO

$$\text{FIFO} = \frac{\text{Current cost only}}{\text{Equivalent units}}$$

7.3.2   Weighted Average

$$\text{Weighted average} = \frac{\text{Beginning cost} + \text{Current cost}}{\text{Equivalent units}}$$

7.4   Spoilage

Equivalent units added for a month are usually less than the actual units added during the month as a result of problems with the production process. This is the result of spoilage or shrinkage, which is usually factored in automatically. There are two types of spoilage:

- **Normal spoilage:** This occurs under regular operating conditions and is charged to factory overhead (inventory cost).

- **Abnormal spoilage:** This does not occur under normal operating conditions and is treated as a period expense. Examples of abnormal spoilage include floods, fire damage, and spoilage materially in excess of standard caused by inefficient equipment or labor.

Question 3 MCQ-09246

On May 1, Mass Manufacturing had 100 units in its beginning work-in-process that were 60 percent complete. The company completed 500 units during May and had 200 units in its ending inventory on May 31 that were 40 percent complete. Using FIFO or weighted average, the equivalent units of production would be:

	Weighted Average	*FIFO*
1.	520	580
2.	580	520
3.	560	620
4.	620	560

Question 4 MCQ-09177

Penn Manufacturing Corporation uses a process costing system to manufacture printers for PCs. The following information summarizes operations for its NoToner model during the quarter ending September 30, Year 1:

	Units	*Direct Labor*
Work-in-process inventory, July 1	100	$ 50,000
Started during the quarter	500	
Completed during the quarter	400	
Work-in-process inventory, September 30	200	
Costs added during the quarter		$ 775,000

Beginning work-in-process inventory was 50 percent complete for direct labor. Ending work-in-process inventory was 75 percent complete for direct labor. What is the total value of the direct labor in the ending work-in-process inventory using the weighted average method?

1. $183,000
2. $194,000
3. $225,000
4. $210,000

8 Activity-Based Costing (ABC)

8.1 Defined

Activity-based costing (ABC) is a costing system that divides production into activities where costs are accumulated (cost pools) and allocated to the product based on the level of activity demanded by the product.

8.2 Characteristics

ABC tends to increase both the number of cost pools (e.g., production orders, material handling, etc.) and allocation bases (e.g., number of production orders, pounds, etc.), whereas a traditional cost system would use one cost base and one allocation base (e.g., factory overhead/direct labor hours).

8.3 Service Cost Allocation

When using ABC, companies may allocate service department costs to production or user departments and ultimately the final products produced. Service costs may be allocated using the direct method or step-down method.

8.3.1 Direct Method

Under the direct method, each service department's total costs are allocated to the production departments directly without recognizing that service departments themselves may also use the services from other service departments.

8.3.2 Step-Down Method

Under the step-down method, service department costs are allocated to production departments as well as other service departments that use a given service department's services. The allocation to other service departments is done through a step-down allocation process.

Question 5 MCQ-09228

Nobis Company uses an ABC system. Which of the following statements is/are correct with respect to ABC?

I. Departmental costing systems are a refinement of ABC systems.

II. ABC systems are useful in manufacturing, but not in merchandising or service industries.

III. ABC systems can eliminate cost distortions because ABC develops cost drivers that have a cause-and-effect relationship with the activities performed.

1. I, II, and III are correct.

2. II and III only are correct.

3. III only is correct.

4. None of the listed choices are correct.

---

9 Joint Product Costing and By-product Costing

In joint product costing (JPC), two or more products are produced from the same common raw material. Joint product costing methods are used to segregate costs associated with each product jointly produced by the same process. Examples include the fuel refining process that produces various octane levels, and lumber processing that produces construction and nonconstruction-grade products.

9.1 Relative Sales Value at Split-off Approach

Joint costs are allocated to joint products based on the relative sales value at split-off.

9.1.1 Example

Joint costs $1,000	
Product A: Sales value at split-off	$10,000
Product B: Sales value at split-off	$30,000
Total	$40,000

2 Computation

1/4 of the $1,000 joint costs, or $250, is assigned to Product A, and $1,000 joint costs, or $750, is assigned to Product B.

9.2   Net Realizable Value Approach

Costs added after the split-off point (separable costs) must be subtracted from the final selling price to arrive at the net realizable value (NRV).

9.2.1   Example

Joint costs $6,000		NRV
Product A: Final selling price $12,000, after split-off cost $2,000	=	$10,000
Product B: Final selling price $25,000, after split-off cost $5,000	=	$20,000
Total		$30,000

9.2.2   Computation

Hence, the NRV of Product A is $10,000 and Product B is $20,000. Therefore, 1/3 of the $6,000 joint costs, or $2,000, would be assigned to Product A, and 2/3 of the $6,000 joint costs, or $4,000, would be assigned to Product B.

9.3   Service Departments Cost Allocation to Joint Products

Service department costs are allocated to joint products based on the joint products proportional unit-volume relationship.

9.3.1   Example

The janitorial service department provides services for Products A and B. The department incurs costs of $6,000, which are allocated to each product based on the joint products unit-volume relationship.

Product A	10,000 gal
Product B	20,000 gal
Total	30,000 gal

Janitorial service department costs are allocated as follows:

Product A: (10,000/30,000) × $6,000	$2,000
Product B: (20,000/30,000) × $6,000	$4,000
Total	$6,000

9.4   By-products

By-products represent outputs of minor value incidental to a manufacturing process. Accounting can take one of two forms:

1. Revenue applied to the main product as a cost reduction

2. Miscellaneous income

Question 6   MCQ-09077

Dallas Company produces joint products, TomL and JimmyJ, each of which incurs separable production costs after the split-off point. Information concerning a batch produced at a $200,000 joint cost before split-off follows:

Product	Separable Costs	Sales Value
TomL	$10,000	$ 80,000
JimmyJ	20,000	50,000
	$30,000	$130,000

What is the joint cost assigned to TomL if costs are assigned using relative net realizable value?

1. $60,000
2. $140,000
3. $48,000
4. $200,000

Question 7   MCQ-09240

Houston Corporation has two products, Astros and Texans, with the following volume information:

	Volume
Product Astros	20,000 gal
Product Texans	10,000 gal
Total	30,000 gal

The joint cost to produce the two products is $120,000. What portion of the joint cost will each product be allocated if the allocation is performed by volume?

1. $100,000 and $0
2. $80,000 and $40,000
3. $40,000 and $80,000
4. $50,000 and $50,000

1 Business Process Management

- Business process management is also known as BPM and promotes continuous improvement in business processes.

- There are many generic BPM methodologies, but the most recognized method is **P**lan, **D**o, **C**heck, **A**ct (**PDCA**).

- Measures can be financial or nonfinancial and should correlate directly to the managed process to determine progress toward expectations.

- Benefits of process management include improved efficiency, effectiveness, and agility for the organization.

2 Shared Services, Outsourcing, and Offshore Operations

- Shared services is a consolidation of redundant services in an organization or group of affiliates. While consolidation of redundant services leads to efficiency, it may result in service flow disruption or failure demand. Shared services is an "in-house" solution.

- Outsourcing services involves contracting with a third party to provide a service. Risks pertaining to outsourcing services include inferior quality of service and the security of information, which may be compromised.

- Offshore operations is the outsourcing of services to providers outside of the country. All outsourcing risks plus lack of control caused by proximity issues and language barriers are potential risks.

3 Selecting and Implementing Improvement Initiatives

- Rational and irrational methods may be used to select improvement initiatives.

- Rational assessments are structured and systematic, while irrational methods are intuitive and emotional.

Question 1   MCQ-09722

Failure demand is:

1. The concept that some modest amount of failure is allowed in a manufacturing process because the cost of zero-error-rate is too high.

2. Demand for a company's product due to the inferior quality and subsequent failure of a competitor's product.

3. Demand for services in a shared-service environment due to failure to provide quality service to the customer the first time.

4. Demand for parts and supplies inventory to support the provision of warranty repairs.

---

4 Business Process Reengineering

- Business process reengineering (BPR) seeks radical change by entirely changing the design and operation of business processes.

- BPR is different from business process management (BPM). BPM seeks incremental rather than radical changes.

- The basic idea behind BPR is to create a fresh start by effectively "wiping the slate clean" and reassessing the process from the ground up.

5 Management Philosophies and Techniques for Performance Improvement

5.1 Just-in-Time (JIT)

The concept of Just-in-Time (JIT) inventory systems is that resources will be introduced to the manufacturing process only as they are needed. An item is produced only when it is requested further downstream in the production cycle. JIT systems serve to make organizations more efficient and better managed. JIT assumes that maintaining inventory does not add value.

5.2 Quality (Control)

Quality is broadly defined by the marketplace as a product's ability to meet or exceed customer expectations. The cost of quality is classified into two components: conformance costs and nonconformance costs.

5.2.1 Conformance Costs

Conformance costs are incurred to ensure quality standards are being met and are classified as either prevention costs or appraisal costs.

- Appraisal costs are costs incurred to discover and remove defective parts before shipment. Examples include statistical quality checks, testing, and inspection.

- Prevention costs are costs incurred to prevent the production of defective units. Examples include employee training, inspection, redesigning products and processes, and searching for higher-quality suppliers.

5.2.2 Nonconformance Costs

Nonconformance costs are the costs associated with not conforming to quality standards and are classified as internal failure costs or external failure costs.

- Internal failure costs are necessary to cure a defect discovered before the product is sent to the customer. Examples include rework labor costs, scrap, tooling changes, disposal costs, cost of a lost unit, and downtime.

- External failure costs are necessary to cure a defect discovered after the product is sent to the customer. Examples include warranty costs, costs for returning the good, liability claims, lost customers, and reengineering.

5.2.3 Total Quality Management

Total quality management (TQM) is an organizational commitment to customer-focused performance that stresses both quality and continuous improvement.

5.3 Lean Manufacturing

Lean manufacturing uses only those resources that are necessary to meet customer requirements or that add value to the production process.

- The focus is also on waste reduction and efficiency.

- Kaizen refers to continuous improvement efforts that improve the efficiency and effectiveness of organizations through greater operational control. Kaizen occurs at the manufacturing stage where the ongoing search for cost reductions takes the form of analysis of production processes to ensure that resource uses stay within target costs.

- An organization may implement process improvements by using activity-based costing (ABC) and activity-based management (ABM).

5.4 Demand Flow

Demand flow seeks to reduce waste by bringing resources into production as they are demanded rather than as they are scheduled for production. Demand flow blends the efficiencies of JIT with the effectiveness (customer-focused, value-added) goals of lean manufacturing.

5.5   Theory of Constraints

Theory of constraints (TOC) is a management philosophy that says organizations are impeded from achieving objectives by the existence of one or more constraints. The organization or project must be consistently operated in a manner that either works around or leverages the constraint. There are five steps to applying TOC:

1. **Identification of the Constraint:** Use of process charts or interviews results in identification of the constraint that produces suboptimal performance.

2. **Exploitation of the Constraint:** Planning around the constraint uses capacity that is potentially wasted by making or selling the wrong products, improper procedures in scheduling, etc.

3. **Subordinate Everything Else to the Above Decisions:** Management directs its efforts to improving the performance of the constraint.

4. **Elevate the Constraint:** Add capacity to overcome the constraint.

5. **Return to the First Step:** Reexamine the process to optimize the results. Remain cognizant that inertia can be a constraint.

5.6   Six Sigma

Six Sigma recommends the use of rigorous metrics in the evaluation of goal achievement and logically anticipates methodologies to improve current processes and develop new processes.

- Existing product and business process improvements (**DMAIC**)
  - **D**efine the problem
  - **M**easure key aspects of the current process
  - **A**nalyze data
  - **I**mprove or optimize current processes
  - **C**ontrol

- New product or business process development (**DMADV**)
  - **D**efine design goals
  - **M**easure CTQ (critical to quality issues)
  - **A**nalyze design alternatives
  - **D**esign optimization
  - **V**erify the design

Question 2   MCQ-09721

Jordan Inc. has adopted a new manufacturing management philosophy that requires that an item is produced only when it is requested downstream in the production cycle. Jordan has adopted which of the following?

1. Business process outsourcing
2. Shared services
3. Just-in-time inventory systems
4. DMAIC

1 Budgets

1.1 Master Budgets

A master budget is a budget at one level of activity.

1.1.1 Design

A master budget (often referred to as a "static" budget) generally includes operating budgets and financial budgets.

1.1.2 Characteristics

The annual plan anticipates the coming year's activities that will contribute to the accomplishment of the long-term and short-term goals outlined in the company's strategic plan.

1.2 Flexible Budgets

Flexible budgets are budgets at several levels of activity.

1.2.1 Design

Flexible budgets are normally designed for a period of one year or less to accommodate the potential changing relationship between per unit revenues and costs.

1.2.2 Characteristics

Flexible budgets include consideration of revenue per unit, variable costs per unit, and fixed costs over the relevant range.

Question 1   MCQ-09219

Fulton Corporation manufactures and sells boxes of fish sticks. The static (master) budget and the actual results for May Year 1 were as follows:

	Actual	Static Budget
Unit sales	24,000	20,000
Sales	$264,000	$200,000
Variable costs of sales	158,400	120,000
Contribution margin	105,600	80,000
Fixed costs	(60,000)	(60,000)
Operating income	$ 45,600	$ 20,000

The operating income for Fulton Corporation using a flexible budget for May Year 1 was:

1. $36,000
2. $42,000
3. $38,000
4. $32,000

2 Operating vs. Financial Budgets

2.1 Operating Budgets

Operating budgets consist of the following budgets:

- Sales budgets
- Production budgets
  - Direct materials budget
  - Direct labor budget
  - Factory overhead budget
  - Cost of goods sold budget
- Selling and administrative budgets

2.2 Financial Budgets

Financial budgets consist of the following budgets:

- Pro forma financial statements
- Cash budgets

Question 2   MCQ-09227

Budgets can be developed under any number of assumptions or methods. Which of the following statements regarding budgeting methods is true?

1. Variance analysis is not possible with a master budget.

2. Master budgets can only be constructed using an annual plan.

3. Flexible budgets are synonymous with variance analysis from standards.

4. Budgeting generally starts with sales forecasts.

Question 3   MCQ-09178

The Bronx Corporation is a manufacturing company with a budgeting system that includes a master budget and flexible budgets for various levels of production. Which of the following statements is/are correct?

I. Master budgets are normally confined to a single year for a single level of activity.

II. Flexible budgets are financial plans prepared in a manner that allows for adjustments for changes in production or sales and accurately reflects expected costs for the adjusted output.

III. Normally, the first step in the preparation of Bronx's master budget for a year would be the preparation of its production budget.

IV. The success of Bronx's budgeting program will depend on the degree to which its top management accepts the program and how its management uses the budgeted data.

1. I, II, and III are correct.

2. I, II, and IV are correct.

3. I and II only are correct.

4. All of the listed choices are correct.

3 Cash Budgets

A typical cash budget will be presented in the format:

> Beginning cash balance
>
> + Cash collections
> _____
>
> Total cash available
>
> - Cash payments
> _____
>
> Ending cash balance (before financing)
>
> + Financing (borrowings less interest payments less repayments)
> _____
>
> Ending cash balance (after financing)

Question 4   MCQ-09199

Rolling Wheels purchases bicycle components in the month prior to assembling them into bicycles. Assembly is scheduled one month prior to budgeted sales. Rolling pays 75% of component costs in the month of purchase and 25% of the costs in the following month. Component costs included in budgeted cost of sales are:

April	May	June	July	August
$ 5,000	$ 6,000	$ 7,000	$ 8,000	$ 8,000

What is Rolling's budgeted cash payments for components in May?

1. $5,750
2. $6,750
3. $7,750
4. $8,000

---

4 Variance Analysis

4.1 Variance Analysis
Variance analysis involves differences between budgeted (targeted or standard) and actual performance.

- Actual cost lower than standard produces a favorable variance.
- Actual cost higher than standard produces an unfavorable variance.

4.2 Expense Variances
Expense variances are calculated for:

- Direct material
- Direct labor
- Manufacturing overhead

4.3 Direct Materials and Direct Labor Variance
For direct materials and direct labor, two variances are calculated:

- Price and quantity variance
- Rate and efficiency variance

EQUATION FORMAT

DM price variance = Actual quantity purchased × (Actual price − Standard price)

DM quantity usage variance = Standard price × (Actual quantity used − Standard quantity allowed)

DL rate variance = Actual hours worked × (Actual rate − Standard rate)

DL efficiency variance = Standard rate × (Actual hours worked − Standard hours allowed)

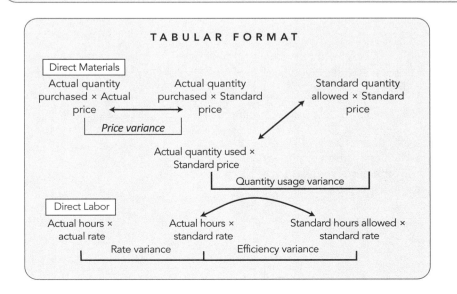

TABULAR FORMAT

4.4 Manufacturing Overhead Variance

Overhead variances represent the analysis of any balance in the overhead account after overhead has been applied. Overapplied overhead (more credit) is favorable, while underapplied overhead (more debit) is unfavorable. The equations for the four overhead variances are as follows:

4.4.1 Variable Overhead Rate (Spending) Variance

VOH rate (spending) variance = Actual hours x (Actual rate − Standard rate)

Assuming a cost driver of labor hours, given the actual number of labor hours that were needed to produce a deliverable, this variance tells managers whether more or less was spent on variable overhead than what was expected.

4.4.2 Variable Overhead Efficiency (Usage) Variance

$$\text{VOH efficiency (usage) variance} = \text{Standard rate} \times \left(\begin{array}{c} \text{Actual} \\ \text{hours} \end{array} - \begin{array}{c} \text{Standard hours allowed for} \\ \text{actual production volume} \end{array} \right)$$

The efficiency variance isolates the amount of total variable overhead variance that is due to using more or fewer labor hours than what was budgeted.

4.4.3 Fixed Overhead Budget (Spending) Variance

FOH budget (spending) variance = Actual fixed overhead − Budgeted fixed overhead

Companies budget an amount for fixed overhead costs every period, and this variance focuses at a high level on whether more or less was spent than budgeted.

4.4.4 Fixed Overhead Volume Variance

FOH volume variance = Budgeted fixed overhead − Standard fixed overhead cost allocated to production*

* based on Actual production x Standard rate

Fixed overhead costs are typically applied using a rate derived from budgeted fixed overhead costs and expected volume (the cost driver). When the actual volume produced differs from the amount used to calculate the fixed overhead application rate, there will be a variance.

4.5   Sales Variances

For sales variances:

- Actual sales prices higher (lower) than budgeted sales prices produce a favorable (unfavorable) variance.

- Actual units sold higher (lower) than budgeted units sold produce a favorable (unfavorable) variance.

4.5.1   Sales Price Variance (or Sales Revenue Flexible Budget Variance)

The sales price variance measures the aggregate impact of a selling price different from budget.

> Sales price variance = (Actual SP per unit − Budgeted SP per unit) x Actual sold units

4.5.2   Sales Volume Variance

The sales volume variance is a flexible budget variance that distills volume activity from other sales performance components. The basic sales volume variance is as follows:

$$\text{Sales volume variance} = \left(\begin{array}{c} \text{Actual} \\ \text{units sold} \end{array} - \begin{array}{c} \text{Budgeted} \\ \text{unit sales} \end{array} \right) \times \text{Standard contribution margin per unit}$$

Question 5	MCQ-09088

Flatbush Corporation has a standard costing system for each of its products. The standard direct material cost to produce a unit of its premier product Brook is 4 pounds of material at $2.50 per pound, or $10.00 per unit. During May Year 1, 8,400 pounds of material costing $20,160 were purchased and used to produce 2,000 units of Brook.

What was the materials usage variance for May Year 1?

1. $1,000 unfavorable.
2. $1,000 favorable.
3. $1,600 unfavorable.
4. $960 unfavorable.

Question 6   MCQ-09098

Bedford Corporation produces 2,500 units of its broadband router each month. Each unit is expected to require 4 labor hours at a cost of $10 per hour. Total labor cost was $104,500 for 9,500 hours worked.

What is the labor rate variance for the production of the router?

1. $10,000 favorable.
2. $10,000 unfavorable.
3. $9,500 favorable.
4. $9,500 unfavorable.

Question 7   MCQ-09118

Norwood Corporation produces a single product. The standard costs for one unit of its Bedford product are as follows:

Direct materials (6 pounds at $0.50 per pound)	$ 3
Direct labor (2 hours at $10 per hour)	20
Variable manufacturing overhead (2 hours at $5 per hour)	10
Total	$ 33

During October Year 2, 4,000 units of Bedford were produced. The costs associated with October operations were as follows:

Material purchased (36,000 pounds at $0.60 per pound)	$ 21,600
Material used in production (28,000 pounds)	
Direct labor (8,200 hours at $9.75 per hour)	79,950
Variable manufacturing overhead incurred	41,820

What is the variable overhead spending variance for Bedford for October Year 2?

1. $4,200 favorable.
2. $820 unfavorable.
3. $1,820 unfavorable.
4. $1,000 unfavorable.

5 Responsibility Segments

Responsibility segments, sometimes referred to as strategic business units (SBUs), are highly effective in establishing accountability for financial dimensions of the business. Performance reporting for each SBU measures financial responsibility. SBUs are often subdivided into additional categories, including product lines, geographic areas, or customers. Specific SBU classifications include:

5.1 Cost SBU

Managers are held responsible for controlling costs in a cost SBU.

5.2 Revenue SBU

Managers are held responsible for generating revenues in a revenue SBU.

5.3 Profit SBU

Managers are held responsible for producing a target profit (i.e., accountability for both revenue and costs) in a profit SBU.

5.4 Investment SBU

Managers are held responsible for the return on the assets invested in an investment SBU. The return must be equal to or greater than the management's minimum required rate of return.

Question 8 MCQ-09128

Elmhurst Corporation is considering changes to its responsibility accounting system. Which of the following statements is/are correct for a responsibility accounting system?

I. In a cost SBU, managers are responsible for controlling costs but not revenue.

II. The idea behind responsibility accounting is that a manager should be held responsible for those items, and only those items, that the manager can actually control to a significant extent.

III. To be effective, a good responsibility accounting system must provide for both planning and control. Planning without control and control without planning is not effective.

IV. Common costs that are allocated to a SBU are normally controllable by the SBU's management.

   1. I and II only are correct.

   2. II and III only are correct.

   3. I, II, and III are correct.

   4. I, II, and IV are correct.

6 Balanced Scorecards

The balanced scorecard (generally a senior management or executive tool) is a control mechanism that gathers information on multiple dimensions of an organization's performance defined by critical success factors necessary to accomplish firm strategy. Critical success factors can be classified within various categories and are commonly displayed as:

6.1 Financial Performance

This category includes critical financial performance measures, such as the current ratio or gross margin.

6.2 Internal Business Processes

This category includes critical business process measures, such as through-put time.

6.3 Customer Satisfaction

This category includes critical customer satisfaction measures, such as customer retention.

6.4 Advancement of Innovation and Human Resource Development

This category includes critical learning and growth measures, such as employee retention, innovations, suggestions made and accepted, etc.

Question 9   MCQ-09138

Canarsie Corporation uses a balanced scorecard to evaluate its digital camera manufacturing operation. Which of the following statements with respect to balanced scorecards is/are correct?

I.   A balanced scorecard reports management information regarding organizational performance in achieving goals classified by critical success factors to demonstrate that no single dimension of organizational performance can be relied upon to evaluate success.

II. Performance measures used in a balanced scorecard tend to be divided into financial, customer, internal business process, and learning and growth.

III. In a balanced scorecard, internal business processes are what the company does in its attempts to satisfy customers.

    1. I and II only are correct.

    2. II and III only are correct.

    3. III only is correct.

    4. I, II, and III are correct.

Forecasting and Projection

1 Absorption (Full) vs. Variable (Direct) Costing

The absorption costing method is a U.S. GAAP basis calculation of gross profit, while variable costing develops contribution margins compatible with breakeven analysis. Variable costing is not allowed for financial reporting purposes under U.S. GAAP.

1.1 Assumptions

General assumptions of cost-volume-profit (CVP) analysis include:

- Costs are either variable or fixed, with volume the only relevant factor affecting cost.
- In relation to production volume, all costs behave in a linear fashion.
- Over the relevant range of production volume, cost behaviors will remain constant.
- The longer (shorter) the time period, the greater the percentage of variable (fixed) costs.

1.2 Absorption (Full Costing) Approach

Absorption costing capitalizes fixed factory overhead as part of inventory in accordance with GAAP. Therefore, absorption costing includes direct materials, direct labor, and fixed and variable overhead.

Revenue	XXX
Less: Cost of goods sold	(XXX)
Gross profit	XXX
Less: Operating expenses	(XXX)
Net income	XXX

1.3 Variable (Direct Costing) Approach

In variable (direct) costing, only variable manufacturing costs (direct materials, direct labor, and variable factory overhead) are included in inventory. Fixed factory overhead is excluded from inventory and treated as a period cost:

Sales	XXX
Less: Variable costs	(XXX)
Contribution margin	XXX
Less: Fixed costs	(XXX)
Net income	XXX

1.4 Income Effect

Relationship Between Production and Sales for the Period	Effect on Inventories	Relationship Between Absorption and Variable Costing Net Incomes
Production = Sales	No change in inventories	Absorption costing net income = Variable costing net income
Production > Sales	Inventory increase	Absorption costing net income* > Variable costing net income
Production < Sales	Inventory decrease	Absorption costing net income** < Variable costing net income

* Net income is higher under absorption costing because fixed manufacturing overhead cost is deferred in inventory as inventories increase.

** Net income is lower under absorption costing because fixed manufacturing overhead cost is released from inventory as inventories decrease.

Question 1   MCQ-09215

Omni Inc. planned and actually manufactured 200,000 units of its single product in its first year of operation. Variable manufacturing costs were $30 per unit of product. Planned and actual fixed manufacturing costs were $600,000, and selling and administrative costs totaled $400,000 in Year 1. Omni sold 120,000 units of product in Year 1 at a selling price of $40 per unit.

Omni's Year 1 operating income using variable costing is:

1. $200,000
2. $440,000
3. $800,000
4. $600,000

2 Breakeven Analysis

Breakeven analysis determines the sales required (in dollars or units) to result in zero profit or loss from operations. After breakeven has been achieved, each additional unit sold will increase net income by the amount of the contribution margin per unit.

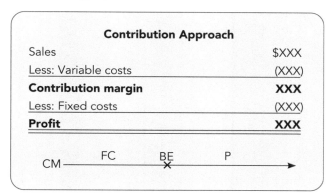

Contribution Approach

Sales	$XXX
Less: Variable costs	(XXX)
Contribution margin	**XXX**
Less: Fixed costs	(XXX)
Profit	**XXX**

2.1 Standard Formulas

2.1.1 Breakeven Point in Units

$$\frac{\text{Total fixed costs}}{\text{Contribution margin per unit}} = \text{Breakeven point in units}$$

2.1.2 Breakeven Point in Dollars

- Multiply the selling price per unit by the breakeven units:

$$\text{Unit price} \times \text{Breakeven point in units} = \text{Breakeven point in dollars}$$

- Contribution margin ratio approach:

$$\frac{\text{Total fixed costs}}{\text{Contribution margin ratio*}} = \text{Breakeven point in dollars}$$

* Contribution margin ratio = Contribution margin/Sales

2.2 Required Sales for a Desired Profit

Breakeven analysis can be extended to calculate the required sales to produce a desired pretax income by treating the desired profit as another fixed cost.

2.2.1 Required Sales in Units

$$\text{Required sales (units)} = \frac{\text{Total fixed cost } + \text{ Desired profit}}{\text{C/M per unit}}$$

2.2.2 Required Sales in Dollars

$$\text{Required sales (\$)} = \frac{\text{Total fixed cost } + \text{ Desired profit}}{\text{C/M\%}}$$

2.3 Breakeven Chart

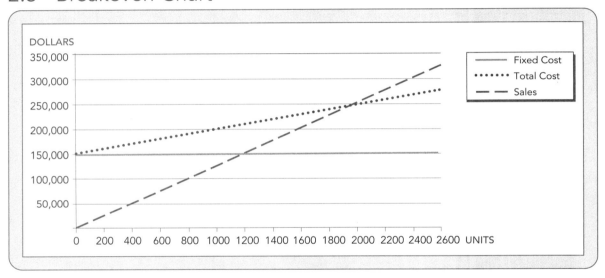

2.4 Margin of Safety

The margin of safety is the excess of sales over breakeven sales.

■ The margin of safety expressed in dollars is calculated as follows:

Total sales in dollars − Breakeven sales in dollars = Margin of safety in dollars

■ The margin of safety can also be expressed as a percentage of sales:

$$\frac{\text{Margin of safety in dollars}}{\text{Total sales}} = \text{Margin of safety percentage}$$

2.5 Target Costing

Target costing is used to establish the product cost allowed that ensures both total sales volume and profitability per unit. With target pricing, the selling price of the product will determine the production costs allowed. The target cost will be equal to the market price less the required profit.

Lampassas Corporation manufactures product Lam at its manufacturing facility. At annual sales of $900,000 for Year 1, product Lam had the following unit sales price and costs:

Sales price	$20
Prime cost	6
Manufacturing overhead	
Variable	1
Fixed	7
Selling & administrative costs	
Variable	1
Fixed	3
	18
Profit	$ 2

What was product Lam's breakeven point in dollars?

1. $500,000
2. $750,000
3. $630,000
4. $900,000

3 Transfer Pricing

3.1 Non-Global Perspective

A transfer price is the price charged for the sale/purchase of a product internally (between two divisions within one overall company). Prices are set based on the following strategies: negotiated price, market price, and cost.

3.2 Global Perspective

Transfer pricing is a methodology for allocating profits or losses among related entities within the same corporation (or legal group) in different tax jurisdictions. Transfer prices should approximate the prices for comparable transactions between unrelated parties. Comparability may be assessed using the following strategies:

1. Transactional methods (comparable uncontrolled price, resale price, gross margin, cost plus).

2. Profitability methods (comparable profits, transactional net margin, comparable profit split, residual profit split).

4 Special Orders

Special order decisions are defined as generally infrequent opportunities that require the firm to decide if a special order should be accepted or rejected. Generally, most direct and variable costs are considered as well as incremental costs.

4.1 Presumed Excess Capacity

- Compare the incremental (additional) costs of the order to the incremental (additional) revenue generated by the order. This process compares the variable cost per unit to the revenue generated per unit.

- Provided the selling price per unit is greater than the variable cost per unit, the contribution margin will increase and the special order should be accepted.

- Fixed costs are sunk and will not be relevant to these decisions.

4.2 Presumed Full Capacity

- Extend the analysis described above to include opportunity cost.

- The opportunity cost will be the contribution margin that would have been produced if the special order were not accepted.

- The production that is forfeited to produce the special order is referred to as the next best alternative use of the facility.

5 Make or Buy Decisions

Similar to accepting or rejecting a special order, managers must consider capacity and, where appropriate, opportunity costs.

5.1 Excess Capacity

If there is excess capacity, the cost of making the product internally is the cost that will be avoided (or saved) if the product is not made. This will be the maximum outside purchase price. Compare variable costs to the purchase price and select the cheapest alternative.

5.2 No Excess Capacity

If there is no excess capacity, the cost of making the product internally is the cost that will be avoided (saved) if the product is not made plus the opportunity cost associated with the decision. Compare the variable costs plus opportunity cost to the purchase price and select the cheapest alternative.

5.3 First Use Existing Capacity Efficiently

Make-or-buy decisions attempt to use existing capacity as efficiently as possible before purchasing from an outside supplier.

Question 3   MCQ-09245

The Harbor Company currently makes 10,000 bolts a year for $50,000. The Cove Corporation has offered to sell Harbor the bolts for $4.00 a piece. Harbor has the cost structure shown below:

	Total	Per Unit
Direct Material	$ 5,000	$0.50
Direct Labor	15,000	1.50
Variable factory overhead	10,000	1.00
Fixed factory overhead	20,000	2.00
Total	$50,000	$5.00

Upon further analysis, Harbor notes that the company can eliminate the services of a $15,000 per year supervisor accounted for in fixed factory overhead if they elect to buy. Harbor's decision to make or buy would result in a comparison of the purchase price of $4.00 to a production cost of:

1. $2.00
2. $3.00
3. $4.50
4. $5.00

---

6 Sell or Process Further

Management's decision as to whether to sell at the split-off point involves comparing the incremental revenues and incremental costs generated after the split-off point. Separable costs (incurred after split-off) are relevant, while joint costs (incurred prior to split-off) are not relevant.

- **Sell:** Incremental costs > Incremental revenues.
- **Process Further:** Incremental revenues > Incremental costs.

7 Keep or Drop a Segment

The decision to keep or drop a segment involves comparing the lost contribution margin to avoidable fixed costs if the segment is dropped. Avoidable fixed costs go away if the segment is dropped and are therefore relevant. Unavoidable fixed costs will be reallocated to other products and continue to be incurred by the company even if the segment is dropped, therefore making them irrelevant.

- **Keep:** Lost contribution margin > Avoidable fixed costs.
- **Drop:** Avoidable fixed costs > Lost contribution margin.

8 Regression Analysis

Linear regression is a method for studying the relationship between two or more variables. Using regression analysis, variation in the dependent variable is explained using one or more independent variables. The dependent variable is specified to be a linear function of one or more independent variables.

8.1 Simple Linear Regression vs. Multiple Linear Regression Analysis

Simple regression involves only one independent variable. Multiple regression analysis involves more than one independent variable. The simple linear regression model takes the following form:

$$y = a + bx$$

Total cost = Fixed cost + Variable rate (units)

Question 4   MCQ-09231

The primary difference between simple linear regression and multiple linear regression is:

1. Multiple linear regression analysis involves more that one independent variable while simple linear regression only considers one independent variable.

2. Multiple linear regression analysis considers the impact of one independent variable on multiple dependent variables while simple linear regression analysis only considers one dependent variable.

3. Multiple linear regression analysis considers the impact of multiple independent variables on multiple dependent variables while simple linear regression analysis only considers one independent and one dependent variable.

4. Multiple linear regression analysis considers codependent variables while simple linear regression analysis only considers mutually exclusive variables.

---

9 Statistical Measures Used to Evaluate Regression Analysis

9.1 Coefficient of Correlation (r)

The coefficient of correlation measures the strength of the linear relationship between the independent variable (x) and the dependent variable (y). In standard notation, the coefficient of correlation is r. The range of r is from -1.0 to $+1.0$, with a value of -1.0 indicating a perfect negative correlation and a value of 1.0 indicating a perfect positive correlation.

9.2 Coefficient of Determination (R^2)

The coefficient of determination (R^2) may be interpreted as the portion of the total variation in the dependent variable (y) explained by the independent variable (x). Its value lies between zero and one. The higher the R^2, the greater the proportion of the total variation in y that is explained by the variation in x. That is, the higher the R^2, the better the fit of the regression line.

Question 5 MCQ-09168

Ivey Company uses regression analysis in examining its costs. It has determined that there is a correlation coefficient of 0.90 between two variables X and Y. Which of the following statements is correct for a correlation coefficient of 0.90?

1. There is little relationship between X and Y.
2. Variation in X explains 90% of the variation in Y.
3. If X increases, Y will never decrease.
4. If X increases, Y will generally increase.

10 Learning Curve Analysis

Learning curve analysis is based on the idea that per-unit labor hours will decline as workers become more familiar with a specific task or production process.

Example

If workers take 30 hours to produce the first unit of a product, and 18 hours to produce the second unit, the learning curve rate will be 80% [(30+18)/(30+30)] and the average time per unit will be 24 hours.

11 High-Low Method

The high-low point method is used to estimate the fixed and variable portions of cost. It assumes that the differences between costs at the highest and lowest production levels are due directly to variable costs. Variable and fixed costs are calculated as follows:

11.1 Computation of Variable Cost per Unit

$$\frac{\text{Costs at high} - \text{Costs at low}}{\text{Activities at high} - \text{Activities at low}} = \frac{\text{Changes in costs}}{\text{Changes in activities}} = \text{Variable cost per unit}$$

11.2 Computation of Total Fixed Costs

> Total cost − (Variable cost per unit × Activity) = Fixed costs

Question 6
MCQ-09097

Presented below is the production data for the first eight months of the year for the mixed costs incurred by Mouton Corporation:

Month	Cost	Units
January	$14,700	1,800
February	15,200	1,900
March	13,700	1,700
April	14,000	1,600
May	14,300	1,500
June	13,100	1,300
July	12,800	1,100
August	14,600	1,500

Mouton Corporation uses the high-low method to analyze mixed costs. Variable cost per unit and fixed cost are respectively:

	VC	FC
1.	$1.00	$13,100
2.	$3.00	$9,500
3.	$1.00	$12,800
4.	$2.00	$15,200

Notes

Class Question Explanations

Business I 3

Business II 5

Business III 11

Business IV 19

Business V 23

Topic A

QUESTION 1

MCQ-09687

Choice "1" is correct.

An audit committee member may qualify for classification as a financial expert using most any combination of education or experience auditing or preparing financial reports. The member must understand generally accepted accounting principles and how to apply them and understand internal control.

Choice "2" is incorrect. There is no requirement that the audit committee financial expert meet minimum service requirements on the board of directors.

Choice "3" is incorrect. Although the audit committee member qualifying as its financial expert may have technical training and experience as an auditor, that is not a requirement. The audit committee member may qualify under any number of different means.

Choice "4" is incorrect. Disclosure of the financial expert is required.

QUESTION 2

MCQ-09689

Choice "3" is correct.

Risk response is a separate component of the COSO *Enterprise Risk Management—Integrated Framework*, not the *Internal Control—Integrated Framework*.

Choice "1" is incorrect. Control environment is known as the tone at the top and is one of the five components of the COSO *Internal Control—Integrated Framework*.

Choice "2" is incorrect. Risk assessment is one of the five components of the COSO *Internal Control—Integrated Framework*.

Choice "4" is incorrect. Control activities generally describes control policies and procedures and is one of the five components of the COSO *Internal Control—Integrated Framework*.

QUESTION 3

MCQ-09691

Choice "2" is correct.

ERM anticipates the development of strategies that are aligned with individual risk appetites and the willingness to accept risk.

Choice "1" is incorrect. All risk cannot be avoided. Risk avoidance is only one of five responses to risk, which also include reduction, sharing, acceptance, and pursuit.

Choice "3" is incorrect. ERM considers business objectives at all layers of the organization, not purely strategy at the entity level.

Choice "4" is incorrect. Uncertainty can rarely be eliminated. ERM can only help reduce uncertainty.

Topic A

QUESTION 1

MCQ-09189

Choice "3" is correct.

The contractionary phase is characterized by falling economic activity and growth. It follows the "peak." During this phase, firm profits are likely to be falling from their highest levels.

Choice "1" is incorrect. An expansionary phase is characterized by rising economic activity (real GDP) and growth. During this phase, firm profits are likely to be rising as the demand for goods and services increases.

Choice "2" is incorrect. At the point of the trough, the firm is at the low point of economic activity. At this point, firm profits are at their lowest level.

Choice "4" is incorrect. A recovery phase is characterized by an increase in economic activity and a return to the firm's long-term growth trend. During this phase, firm profits generally begin to stabilize as the demand for goods and services begins to rise.

QUESTION 2

MCQ-09112

Choice "4" is correct.

A perfectly competitive market is characterized by: (1) a large number of firms, (2) very little product differentiation (firms sell identical products), and (3) no barriers to market entry.

Choice "1" is incorrect because firms in a perfectly competitive market sell a homogeneous product and, thus, don't compete via product differentiation.

Choice "2" is incorrect by definition. A perfectly competitive market has no barriers to entry.

Choice "3" is incorrect because it describes oligopoly.

QUESTION 3

MCQ-09161

Choice "4" is correct.

Fiscal policy refers to government spending and tax policies. Expansionary fiscal policy consists of increases in government spending and/or decreases in taxes. When the government increases government spending and/or decreases taxes, the aggregate demand curve shifts right. As a result, real GDP increases, leading to an increase in, or expansion of, economic activity.

Business II

Topic B

QUESTION 1 MCQ-09082

Choice "2" is correct.

An increase in production costs shifts the supply curve to the left. As a result, equilibrium price will rise and equilibrium quantity will fall.

Choice "1" is incorrect because an increase in consumer income would shift the demand curve to the right, causing equilibrium quantity to rise.

Choice "3" is incorrect because an increase in the price of a substitute good would shift the demand curve to the right, causing equilibrium quantity to rise.

Choice "4" is incorrect since a decrease in the price of a complementary good would shift demand to the right, causing equilibrium quantity to rise.

QUESTION 2 MCQ-09195

Choice "3" is correct.

When the supply curve shifts to the left, equilibrium price will rise and equilibrium quantity will fall.

Choice "1" is incorrect. Equilibrium price and quantity will increase when the demand curve shifts to the right.

Choice "2" is incorrect. Equilibrium price and quantity will fall when the demand curve shifts to the left.

Choice "4" is incorrect. Equilibrium price will fall and equilibrium quantity will rise when the supply curve shifts to the right.

QUESTION 3 MCQ-09092

Choice "3" is correct.

The price elasticity of demand is defined as:

$$\text{Price elasticity of demand Real GDP} = \frac{\text{\% Change in quantity demanded}}{\text{\% Change in price}}$$

Using the point method of calculating price elasticity of demand, if the price of a product rises from \$5 to \$6 and the demand for that product decreases from 100 pounds to 90 pounds, the price elasticity of demand is calculated as follows:

$$\frac{\text{\% Change in quantity demanded}}{\text{\% Change in price}} = \frac{(90 - 100) / 100}{(\$6 - \$5) / \$5} = \frac{(0.10)}{0.20} = (0.50)$$

Choices "1", "2", and "4" are incorrect per the above explanation.

QUESTION 4 MCQ-09201

Choice "4" is correct.

Strategy is generally influenced by four factors, divided between internal and external factors. Internal factors include an individual firm's strengths and weaknesses, while external factors include opportunities and threats. The discovery of a microbe in the environment that impacts sales is a threat.

Choice "1" is incorrect. Clearly, an external event that reduces sales is not a strength.

Choice "2" is incorrect. The discovery of an external challenge that reduces revenue is a threat, not a weakness.

Choice "3" is incorrect. An external event, as described, that decreases sales is not an opportunity.

QUESTION 5

Choice "1" is correct.

Statement I is correct. Statement I says that cost leadership strategies typically focus on building market share and matching the prices of rival firms *and* that a possible reason for the lack of success of Rivington's cost leadership strategy is that it has an outmoded warehousing and distribution system. Cost leadership strategies certainly focus on building market share and matching prices, and an outmoded warehousing and distribution system could certainly keep a firm from reducing its costs sufficiently.

Statement II is correct. Statement II says that differentiation strategies attempt to gain competitive advantage by creating the perception that products are superior to those of competitors *and* that a reason for the lack of success of Rivington's differentiation strategy is that it implemented its strategy by advertising its "everyday low prices." The definition of differentiation strategies is correct. However, "everyday low prices" is not normally a way to implement a differentiation strategy, and that could have been a reason for the lack of success of the strategy.

Statement III is incorrect. Statement III says that vertical integration strategies attempt to control an entire supply chain *and* that a possible reason for the lack of success of Rivington's strategy is that it had not acquired any of the companies in its supply chain. Acquiring companies is not a necessary factor for the control of a supply chain.

Topic C

QUESTION 1

Choice "3" is correct.

Credit risk relates to a debtor's exposure to either the inability to secure financing or the inability to secure financing at attractive interest rates. Arbor's use of long-term financing locks in financing at predictable rates and is designed to eliminate risk that credit might not be available.

Choice "1" is incorrect. Interest rate risk generally relates to the changes in valuation of investments that result from interest rate fluctuations. Although Arbor Corporation is concerned about changes in interest rates, its concern relates to meeting ongoing credit needs, not the valuation of its instrument.

Choice "2" is incorrect. Market risk relates to nondiversifiable risks associated with participation in the economy. Although the Arbor Corporation is concerned about its appeal in the market place as a borrower, its predominant concern relates to its company-specific business risks that might impede the ability to secure credit to meet ongoing working capital needs.

Choice "4" is incorrect. Default risk represents a creditor's exposure to non-payment. The question relates to the debtor's risk exposure.

QUESTION 2

Choice "4" is correct.

The minimum annual percentage earned by an investment that will cause a company to put money into a particular security or project.

The required rate of return is the risk-free rate plus the financial risks that represent possible exposure to loss plus an inflation premium. Market risk is the possible loss in trading value of assets or liabilities in markets due to the overall performance of the market. Market risk is nondiversifiable. Liquidity risk is the risk of a lack of marketability of an investment that cannot be bought or sold quickly enough to prevent or minimize a loss. Default risk is the possibility that a debtor may not repay the principal or interest due on a timely basis. Inflation premium is the inflation rate for the period, an external economic force that the company cannot control. However, inflation reduces the real return of an investment, so it must be added back to the required rate.

Choices "1", "2", and "3" are incorrect, based on the above explanation.

Business II

QUESTION 3

Choice "4" is correct.

The question asks which of the answer options would *not* serve to improve the exchange rate of the U.S. dollar relative to foreign currencies.

Choice "4" is correct because increased U.S. capital investment in a foreign economy would likely cause the exchange rate for the U.S. dollar to *deteriorate*. Increased capital investment in a foreign country creates a demand for the foreign currency. The increased demand for a fixed amount of foreign currency ultimately increases the value (exchange rate) of the foreign currency relative to the U.S. dollar.

Choice "1" is incorrect because foreign inflation would reduce the buying power of the foreign currency, thereby increasing the value of the U.S. dollar, which caused the exchange rate to *improve*.

Choice "2" is incorrect because declining domestic income will reduce the amount of domestic currency spent. Reduced demand for foreign currency from a declining pool of domestic currency will effectively strengthen the domestic currency and *improve* exchange rates.

Choice "3" is incorrect because low foreign interest rates will reduce incentives for foreign investment. The less demand for foreign currency, the stronger the domestic currency. Exchange rates *improve*.

QUESTION 4

Choice "2" is correct.

Approach: Set up assumed values for transactions and test for appropriate gain or loss.

Receivable

Denominated in yen. Assume the transaction is for 1,000 yen. On the settlement date, there is a foreign exchange gain on the receipt of 1,000 yen. In order for there to be a gain, the 1,000 yen must be worth more dollars than on the transaction date. Therefore, fewer yen must be equal to a dollar (for there to be more dollars), so the number of yen exchangeable into dollars decreased.

Payable

Denominated in euros. Assume the transaction is for 2,000 euros. On the settlement date, there is a foreign exchange loss on the payment of 2,000 euros. For there to be a loss, it must take more dollars to buy the same euros. Therefore, the number of euros exchangeable into dollars must have decreased.

QUESTION 5

Choice "2" is correct.

The question asks which of the series of items describes Hickman International's exposure to economic risks of exchange rate fluctuation.

Economic exposure represents the potential that the present value of an organization's cash flows could increase or decrease as a result of changes in the exchange rate. Economic exposure is generally defined through local currency appreciation or depreciation and measured in relation to the organization's earnings and cash flows.

This choice is correct because net inflows of a depreciated local currency (Canadian dollar) relative to a domestic currency (United States dollar) results in economic loss.

Choice "1" is incorrect because it represents a transaction risk.

Choices "3" and "4" are incorrect because they represent translation risks.

QUESTION 6

Choice "1" is correct.

Future contracts to buy euros would be used to hedge transaction exposure to exchange rate risk for an account payable.

Futures contracts for foreign currency represent the obligation to buy or sell a particular number of foreign currency units at a specific time and at a specific date. Futures contracts are often used to hedge specific contracts, while forward contracts are used to specify general foreign currency needs. Hedge contracts to mitigate risks associated with liabilities are call or buy contracts. The company locks in the amount of foreign currency it needs to satisfy its obligation ensuring that a weakening domestic currency won't make the settlement more expensive.

Choice "2" is incorrect because a futures contract to sell would be applicable to accounts receivable.

Choices "3" and "4" are incorrect because forward contracts would normally not be used in this situation.

Business Final Review

Topic A

QUESTION 1

MCQ-09175

Choice "1" is correct.

Letters of credit are third-party guarantees of obligations incurred by Cash Burn Enterprises. The letter of credit would provide specific assurances to otherwise unsecured creditors that payment is assured, thereby ensuring their consistent cooperation to provide needed supplies.

Choice "2" is incorrect. Lines of credit provide a defined safety net for cash availability, but provide comparatively less assurances that cash flows would be dedicated to specific vendors. A letter of credit (vs. a line of credit) meets the objective of providing specific assurances to vendors.

Choice "3" is incorrect. Subordinated debentures are higher-risk (higher yield) securities that potentially provide cash infusion, but provide comparatively less assurances that cash flows would be dedicated to specific vendors.

Choice "4" is incorrect. Working capital financing is nothing more than using the period allowed by trade creditors to spontaneously finance short-term purchases. Working capital financing is potentially dangerous in circumstances where receipts may lag behind disbursement obligations. Nonpayment can result in default and interruption of supplies. Cash Burn Enterprises would not use this strategy.

QUESTION 2

MCQ-09720

Choice "2" is correct.

Investors and firms both use leverage—operating and financial leverage—in an effort to generate higher profits. However, the use of leverage will magnify losses as well as profits. High operating leverage stems from the use of a high percentage of fixed costs relative to variable costs. Once sales have covered the fixed costs, additional sales (and lower variable costs) will result in higher operating income. The opposite is true for losses; higher operating leverage magnifies losses because the fixed costs still have to be covered even when sales decline. A similar situation occurs with financial leverage, which stems from a higher percentage of debt, rather than equity, financing. Once sales are sufficient to cover the fixed interest payments, additional sales (less variable expenses) will result in higher operating income, which would be available as returns to equity holders.

Choice "1" is incorrect. Financing the firm with a high percentage of long-term debt results in financial leverage. The relative proportion of debt versus equity financing does not affect operating leverage. Operating leverage results from a high percentage of fixed operating costs.

Choice "3" is correct. Using a high degree of both types of leverage increases risk, based on the need to cover the high fixed costs. With the higher risk, you may have higher returns or you may have higher losses, depending on the operating results.

Choice "4" is incorrect. Increasing variable operating expenses decreases operating leverage and does not affect financial leverage. Operating leverage is higher when fixed costs are higher. Financial leverage is higher when the firm uses a higher percentage of long-term debt to finance the operations.

Business III

QUESTION 3

Choice "2" is correct.

The cost of preferred stock is computed as using the formula below with the terms defined below:

Cost of preferred stock = Preferred stock dividends / Net proceeds of preferred stock

Cash dividends on preferred stock (1,000 shares × $50 × 8%)		$ 4,000
Proceeds of preferred stock sale net of fees and costs		
Proceeds (1,000 shares × $52)	$52,000	
Flotation costs	(2,500)	
Net proceeds		$49,500
Cost of preferred stock ($4,000 / $49,500)		8.08%

Choice "1" is incorrect. The cost of preferred stock is computed as the dividend amount divided by the net proceeds (computed as the total amount collected from the sale of the stock issue net of flotation costs, not the par value, net of flotation costs).

Choice "3" is incorrect. The cost of preferred stock is not the stated rate of the issue.

Choice "4" is incorrect. The cost of preferred stock is computed as the dividend amount divided by the net proceeds (computed as the total amount collected from the sale of the stock issue net of flotation costs, not market proceeds prior to consideration of flotation costs).

QUESTION 4

Choice "3" is correct.

The capital asset pricing model for computation of the cost of equity financing (retained earnings) uses the formula below with terms defined as follows:

kre = krf + [bi × (km − krf)]	
krf = risk-free rate of return	**2.00%**
bi = beta coefficient of stock (1.25 / 1.00)	**1.25**
km = market rate	**12.00%**
km − krf = market risk premium (12% − 2%)	**10.00%**
kre = 2% + [1.25 × (12% − 2%)]	
kre = 2% + [1.25 × 10%]	
kre = 2% + [12.50%]	
kre = 14.5%	

Choice "1" is incorrect. The cost of equity capital is not the risk-free rate of return.

Choice "2" is incorrect. The cost of equity capital is not the expected return on the market.

Choice "4" is incorrect. The cost of equity capital is not the market risk premium.

Topic B

QUESTION 1   MCQ-09076

Choice "1" is correct.

Compensating balance arrangements are a mechanism to reduce fees, not to increase the availability of cash. Compensating balances normally decrease the availability of cash since they represent an agreement to maintain a minimum balance in exchange for reduced fees.

Choice "2" is incorrect. Zero-balance accounts are designed to increase the availability of cash. Banking arrangements are made to assume a theoretical zero balance in a particular account and to replenish the account when checks are presented. Maintaining a zero balance in an operating account ensures that cash is invested for the maximum period before disbursement.

Choice "3" is incorrect. Electronic funds transfers expedite deposits. Funds are electronically transferred for deposit without waiting for mail delivery and manual deposit processing by the recipient and the bank.

Choice "4" is incorrect. Lock box systems increase the availability of cash by expediting deposits. Receipts are sent directly to a dedicated mailing address and processed immediately by the bank, thereby skipping the internal deposit processing procedures of the recipient.

QUESTION 2   MCQ-09146

Choice "3" is correct.

Computing the annual interest rate associated with cash discounts is developed as follows:

1. Compute the annualized increment for the discount:
    Days per year ÷ Days outstanding after discount
    $360 \div (30 - 12) = 20$

2. Compute the effective interest rate with discount:
    $2\% \div (100\% - 2\%) = 2.048\%$

3. Multiply the annualized increment by the rate:
    $2.048\% \times 20 = 40.8\%$

Choice "1" is incorrect. Multiplying 2% by 12 months provides the answer of 24% is incorrect per above.

Choice "2" is incorrect. The annualized interest rate for 2/10 net 30 terms is 36.7%. Although these terms are common, the annualized results are not universal.

Choice "4" is incorrect. This response computes the annualized increment for the discount based upon the days during which the discount is effective (12) vs. the days outstanding after the discount (18).

Business III

QUESTION 3

Choice "4" is correct.

Days sales in accounts receivable is calculated using the following formula:

$$\text{Days sales in accounts receivable} = \frac{\text{Ending accounts receivable (net)}}{\text{(Sales (net)} / 365)}$$

For Year 3, XYZ's days sales in accounts receivable can be calculated as follows:

$$\text{Days sales in accounts receivable} = \frac{\$47,000}{(\$730,000 / 365)}$$

$$= 23.50$$

Choices "1", "2", and "3" are incorrect based on the above explanation.

QUESTION 4

Choice "1" is correct.

The optimal inventory order is formulated by the economic order quantity equation shown below with the following term definitions:

EOQ = Economic order quantity

S   = Annual sales in units   2,500

O   = Cost per purchase order $ 1,000

C   = Carrying cost per unit $ 500

$$EOQ = \sqrt{\frac{2SO}{C}}$$

$$EOQ = \sqrt{\frac{2(2,500 \times \$1,000)}{\$500}}$$

$$EOQ = 100$$

Choice "2" is incorrect. The economic order quantity is not equal to the stock-out costs divided by the months of the year. Stock-out costs are irrelevant to economic order quantity.

Choice "3" is incorrect. The economic order quantity is not equal to sales in units divided by the months in the year.

Choice "4" is incorrect. The economic order quantity is not equal to double the stock-out costs divided by the months in the year. Stock-out costs are irrelevant to economic order quantity.

Topic C

QUESTION 1

Choice "4" is correct.

This choice is not an influence on subjective assumptions. Instead, it is an assumption underlying the Black-Scholes method of valuing options.

Choice "1" is incorrect. Generalized rules of thumb are influences on subjective assumptions. Use of rules of thumb is normally considered to be "intuition" rather than objective analysis, a guideline that provides simplified advice regarding a particular subject. Rules of thumb develop as a result of experience rather than theory. An example of a rule of thumb is "always have three to six months of expenses in an emergency fund."

Choice "2" is incorrect. Behavior biases are influences on subjective assumptions. These are usually based on the personality characteristics of the analyst, and also include confirmation bias and illusion of control. Confirmation bias occurs when people filter out potentially useful facts and opinions that do not coincide with their preconceived notions. This causes them to overlook information that disagrees with their own opinions, which could result in poor decisions. Illusion of control occurs when people overestimate their ability to control events over which they really have no actual control.

Choice "3" is incorrect. The effect of loss aversion is an influence on subjective assumptions. This is the tendency to strongly prefer avoiding losses over acquiring gains. According to economics and decision theory, human beings would rather not lose a dollar than to gain a dollar. This leads to loss aversion in decision making, which may not always yield the best result.

QUESTION 2

Choice "2" is correct.

Business losses are generally deemed to be the most emotionally distracting influence on decision makers. The manager's fear of continued losses and aversion to a sure loss can motivate the manager to continue to operate losing projects for too long and thereby magnify losses.

Choice "1" is incorrect. Overconfidence can distort business decisions, but it can be easily countered with analysis rather than the fear that accompanies losses.

Choice "3" is incorrect. Use of available data, particularly the most easily available data, can be used to confirm judgments rather than rigorously challenge decisions. Additional questioning can resolve this issue and more easily be accomplished than overcoming fear of losses.

Choice "4" is incorrect. Excessive optimism can distort decision making, however, this emotion is more easily countered with analysis than the irrational emotion that often accompanies the fear of losses.

Business III

Topic D

QUESTION 1

Choice "2" is correct.

After-tax cash flow is computed as the sum of cash inflows (net of tax) plus the depreciation tax shield afforded by depreciation. After-tax cash flows can be computed in one of two ways:

1. Compute the cash flow after tax and add back the depreciation tax shield:

Cash inflow	$150,000	
@ 1 – tax rate	65%	$ 97,500
Depreciation	50,000	
@ tax rate	35%	17,500
After-tax cash flow		$115,000

2. Compute the taxable cash inflow, compute taxes, and reduce cash inflow by the amount of the taxes.

Cash inflow	$150,000
Depreciation	50,000
Taxable cash inflow	100,000
Tax rate	35%
Taxes	35,000
Cash inflow	$150,000
Taxes	35,000
After-tax cash flow	$115,000

Choice "1" is incorrect. This choice computes cash flows net of depreciation without considering tax effects.

Choice "3" is incorrect. This choice erroneously applies a factor equal to 1 – tax rate to the depreciation tax shield in arriving at the after-tax cash flows.

Choice "4" is incorrect. This choice inappropriately discounts the after-tax cash inflows for all five years.

QUESTION 2

Choice "4" is correct.

The net present value of an investment is the difference between the present value of the investment and the present value of the after-tax cash flows resulting from the investment. In its most straightforward format, the examiners will give you an even stream of after-tax cash flows and the associated discount factors and require computation of the net present value. In this case, the net present value is computed as follows:

Investment			$(150,000)
After-tax cash flows			
Income	$40,000 × 3.791 =	$151,640	
Salvage	$15,000 × 0.621 =	9,315	
Total after-tax cash flows			160,955
Positive net present value			$ 10,955

Choice "1" is incorrect. The discounted cash flows before salvage are positive, not negative, and the answer does not consider salvage.

Choice "2" is incorrect. The discounted cash flows before salvage are only part of the answer. You must also consider salvage.

Choice "3" is incorrect. The discounted value of the salvage is not the net present value.

Cash flows are after taxes. The tax rate is a distracter.

QUESTION 3

Choice "2" is correct.

The payback method is the most simple of all investment evaluation methods. The formula is purely the initial investment divided by the annual cash flows. In this case, the investment is $100,000, and the annual cash flows of $23,850 are used to compute to a payback period of 4.19 years as follows:

$100,000 / $23,850 = 4.19 years

Choice "1" is incorrect. The initial investment is not reduced by the salvage value.

Choice "3" is incorrect. The initial investment is not increased by the salvage value.

Choice "4" is incorrect. This answer is a distracter.

Notes

Topic A

QUESTION 1   MCQ-14518

Choice "3" is correct.

Middle management is responsible for carrying out governance policies.

Choice "1" is incorrect. The board of directors is responsible for setting governance policies.

Choice "2" is incorrect. Executives ensure that an IT governance structure is in place and executed effectively.

Choice "4" is incorrect. End users are responsible for following processes and procedures.

QUESTION 2   MCQ-14519

Choice "1" is correct.

A company's vision statement represents its aspirations and goals.

Choice "2" is incorrect. A corporate strategy shapes an organization's operations and business model.

Choice "3" is incorrect. IT strategy aligns with corporate strategy to achieve its objectives.

Choice "4" is incorrect. A steering committee develops and communicates strategic goals.

Topic B

QUESTION 1   MCQ-14520

Choice "3" is correct.

The outsourcing company loses some control over how the IT functions are performed and grants the outsourced firm access to sensitive information.

Choice "1" is incorrect. Instead of purchasing training for internal employees, outsourcing the IT functions gives organizations access to IT experts on a fractional cost basis. This is an advantage of outsourcing.

Choice "2" is incorrect. If an organization outsources its IT functions, it can spend less time on the complexities of IT and more time on the organization's growth and strategy. This is an advantage of outsourcing.

Choice "4" is incorrect. Outsourcing allows organizations to pay for what they need without large investments in hardware, software, or IT staff. This is an advantage of outsourcing.

QUESTION 2   MCQ-14521

Choice "2" is correct.

B2C e-commerce allows businesses to interface and sell goods directly to their customers.

Choice "1" is incorrect. B2B e-commerce involves the buying and selling of goods and services between business entities.

Choice "3" is incorrect. C2B e-commerce allows consumers to offer their goods or services to a business.

Choice "4" is incorrect. C2C e-commerce functions as an online marketplace in which individual consumers buy and sell goods with each other.

Business IV

Topic C

QUESTION 1

Choice "4" is correct.

Variety refers to the range of data types being processed or analyzed. Here the data includes text, numbers, images, and videos, or a wide range of data types.

Choice "1" is incorrect. Volume represents the quantity or amount of data. No information about the quantity of data is given.

Choice "2" is incorrect. Velocity refers to the speed of data accumulation or data processing. No information about the speed of data accumulation is given.

Choice "3" is incorrect. Veracity represents the reliability, quality, or integrity of the data. No information about the reliability of the data is given.

QUESTION 2

Choice "4" is correct.

Descriptive analytics indicate what happened. Here the average sales are examined. This is what actually happened.

Choice "1" is incorrect. Predictive analytics help forecast future data points. This is not what is happening in this question.

Choice "2" is incorrect. Diagnostic analytics reveal why an event happened. No information about why is given in this question.

Choice "3" is incorrect. Prescriptive analytics reveal how to achieve a desired event. No predictive information is given.

Topic D

QUESTION 1

Choice "4" is correct.

During the planning phase, the organization evaluates the need for a new or improved information system.

Choice "1" is incorrect. During the analysis phase, information is gathered from all vital stakeholders to comprehensively compile and analyze the needs of end users.

Choice "2" is incorrect. During the design phase, the project will start designing the system to meet the agreed-upon user needs.

Choice "3" is incorrect. The technical implementation plan created in prior phases is executed in the develop step.

QUESTION 2

Choice "2" is correct.

Stress testing checks the program to see how well it deals with abnormal resource demands.

Choice "1" is incorrect. Sanity testing exercises the logical reasoning and behavior of the software.

Choice "3" is incorrect. Regression tests rerun test cases within the entire application.

Choice "4" is incorrect. Security testing verifies that authorized access levels function properly.

Topic E

QUESTION 1

Choice "4" is correct.

Physical controls monitor and control the workplace environment and computing facilities. A security system connected to local law enforcement is an example of a physical control.

Choice "1" is incorrect. Authentication controls are an example of logical access controls. Authentication controls verify the identity of individuals accessing the system.

Choice "2" is incorrect. Data encryption is a logical access control. Data encryption involves using a digital key to scramble and decrypt a message.

Choice "3" is incorrect. Digital certificates are logical access controls. Digital certificates are electronic documents that are digitally signed by a trusted party.

QUESTION 2

Choice "2" is correct.

Compliance risk is the risk of not meeting the requirements of regulatory bodies.

Choice "1" is incorrect. Availability risk is the risk that an organization is not able to access and utilize its information technology.

Choice "3" is incorrect. Financial risk is the risk of losing financial resources as a result of misuse.

Choice "4" is incorrect. Strategic risk is the risk of misalignment of business and IT strategies.

Topic A

QUESTION 1

MCQ-09699

Choice "3" is correct.

Drivers would most likely comprehend nonfinancial measures that represent controllable features of their job. In this case, the achievement of a delivery within the time allowed (assuming standards properly consider miles and hours of service) would likely be the most effective metric.

Choice "1" is incorrect. Contribution per mile driven is a financial measure that would be useful for financial managers and even operational managers responsible for financial performance. This metric would not be as effective for drivers, as it does not relate to their job duties in a meaningful way.

Choice "2" is incorrect. Gross margin per mile driven is a financial measure that would be marginally useful since it comingles fixed and variable costs and uses a variable cost driver. However, the significance of the gross margin measure would most likely be lost on drivers.

Choice "4" is incorrect. Although beating standards is generally beneficial, using the wrong standards is potentially dangerous. If standards were computed properly in this instance, a driver could only beat them if he or she speeds or works longer than allowed by Department of Transportation regulations.

QUESTION 2

MCQ-09208

Choice "3" is correct.

ROI equals net income divided by average invested capital. Consequently, ROI equals 27.5% [($311,000 sales − $250,000 VC − $50,000 FC) / $40,000 average invested capital].

QUESTION 3

MCQ-09216

Choice "1" is correct.

Residual income is income of an investment center minus an imputed interest charge for invested capital. Accordingly, Vale's residual income is $144,000 [($500,000 sales − $300,000 VC − $50,000 traceable FC) net income − (6% × $100,000 average invested capital) imputed interest].

Business V

Topic B

QUESTION 1

Choice "2" is correct.

In this question, they want to know which of a series of statements about costs is/are correct. "All of the above" is an available option.

Statement I says that the cost of the raw materials in Applewhite's products is considered a variable cost. The more Applewhite manufactures, the more the total cost of the raw materials will be. Statement I is correct.

Statement II says that the cost of the depreciation of Applewhite's factory machinery is considered a variable cost because Applewhite uses an accelerated depreciation method for both book and income tax purposes. Just because a cost changes over time (which is what using an accelerated depreciation method will cause) does not mean that the cost is variable. The fact that Applewhite may use the same method for book and tax purposes is irrelevant. Statement II is wrong.

Statement III says that the cost of electricity for Applewhite's manufacturing facility is considered a fixed cost, even if the cost of the electricity has both variable and fixed components. The cost of the electricity would be considered a "mixed" cost, not a fixed cost. Statement III is wrong.

QUESTION 2

Choice "2" is correct.

In this question, they want to know the amount of overapplied or underapplied overhead at the end of a month.

For Culpepper, factory overhead is applied based on 40 percent of direct labor cost. Direct labor cost is $400,000, and factory overhead applied would be $160,000. Actual overhead is $175,000. Factory overhead would be underapplied by $15,000.

QUESTION 3

Choice "2" is correct.

The equivalent units of production for weighted average and FIFO are computed as follows:

FIFO

Beg. WIP [Percent **to be** completed; 100 × (1 − 60%)]		40
Units completed	500	
Beginning WIP	(100)	
		400
Ending WIP (Percent completed; 200 × 40%)		80
Equivalent Units		**520**

Weighted Average

Units completed	500
Ending WIP (Percent completed; 200 × 40%)	80
Equivalent Units	**580**

Choice "1" is incorrect. This selection identifies the computation of equivalent units with the wrong method.

Choice "3" is incorrect. This selection computes weighted average and FIFO equivalent units assuming that the percentage of ending inventory completion is consistent with the beginning of the month and, furthermore, reversed the presentation by placing FIFO under weighted average and vice versa.

Choice "4" is incorrect. This selection computes weighted average and FIFO equivalent units assuming that the percentage of ending inventory completion is consistent with the beginning of the month.

QUESTION 4

Choice "3" is correct.

In this question, they want a calculation of ending inventory cost using the weighted average method of process costing. The general approach to this problem is to (1) compute the equivalent units; (2) compute the unit cost of the production; and (3) apply the unit cost to the equivalent units in the ending inventory.

Before computing the equivalent units, it is helpful to reconcile the actual units. 100 units were in beginning inventory and 500 units were started, for a total of 600 units. 400 units were completed and 200 units remained in ending inventory, again for a total of 600 units.

Converting to equivalent units using the weighted-average method, the units completed at 100 percent complete and the units in ending inventory at their percentage of completion are considered. Equivalent units were thus 550 [400 + (200 × 0.75)]. Using the weighted average method, the percentage of completion of the beginning inventory is not considered.

To compute the unit cost of production, the cost of the beginning inventory plus the cost added during the month are considered. The cost of the beginning inventory was $50,000. $775,000 of cost was added during the month, for a total of $825,000 ($50,000 + $775,000). The per equivalent unit cost is $1,500 ($825,000 / 550).

There were 150 equivalent units in ending inventory (200 × 0.75). The cost of this inventory was thus $225,000 ($1,500 × 150).

Business V

QUESTION 5 MCQ-09228

Choice "3" is correct.

In this question, they want to know which of a series of statements is/are correct with respect to ABC.

Statement I says that departmental costing systems are a refinement of ABC systems. Actually, ABC systems are a refinement of departmental costing systems. Statement I is incorrect.

Statement II says that ABC systems are useful in manufacturing, but not in merchandising or service industries. ABC systems are useful in all three of these businesses. Statement II is incorrect.

Statement III says that ABC systems can eliminate cost distortions because ABC develops cost drivers that have a cause-and-effect relationship with the activities performed. Statement III is correct.

QUESTION 6 MCQ-09077

Choice "2" is correct.

In this question, they want to know how much joint cost is allocated to each of two products. Joint cost allocation in this question is based on relative net realizable value (relative net sales value at split-off point), and sales values and separable costs after the split-off point are provided.

Using the relative net realizable value method of allocating joint costs, the net realizable value of both products can be calculated as follows:

	TomL	JimmyJ
Sales	$ 80,000	$ 50,000
Separable costs	(10,000)	(20,000)
Net realizable value	$ 70,000	$ 30,000

The joint cost is allocated based on the percentage of the product's net realizable value to the total. For TomL, that is 70% ($70,000 ÷ $100,000). 70% of the joint cost, or $140,000 ($200,000 × 0.70), is thus allocated to TomL.

30% of the joint cost, or $60,000 ($200,000 × 0.30), is allocated to JimmyJ, but they did not ask that.

QUESTION 7 MCQ-09240

Choice "2" is correct.

In this question, they want to know how much joint cost is allocated to each of two products. Joint cost allocation in this question is based on volume, and volumes are provided.

The total volume is 30,000 gallons. Product Astros has 20,000 gallons (2/3) of the total. Thus Product Astros is allocated $80,000 ($120,000 × 2/3) of the total, and Product Texans is allocated the remaining $40,000 ($120,000 × 1/3).

Business Final Review

Topic C

QUESTION 1

Choice "3" is correct.

Failure demand is the demand for additional services due to the failure of the shared service operation to provide the proper level of service to the customer the first time. It can be viewed as "do over" work, because the inferior service (or product) must be provided again in order to satisfy the appropriate quality standards.

Choice "1" is incorrect. This concept applies to quality programs. Although there are proponents of zero-defect, even Six Sigma allows for some minor number of defects because a zero-defect standard is extremely difficult and costly to attain.

Choice "2" is incorrect. Although this situation might definitely occur, there is no name for it in process or product management.

Choice "4" is incorrect. Failure demand is not related to warranty programs.

QUESTION 2

Choice "3" is correct.

The concept of just-in-time (JIT) inventory systems is that resources will be introduced to the manufacturing process only as they are needed. An item is produced only when it is requested further downstream in the production cycle. JIT systems serve to make organizations more efficient and better managed.

Choice "1" is incorrect. Business process outsourcing involves contracting with a third party to provide a service, such as accounts payable or payroll operations. Risks pertaining to outsourcing services include inferior quality of service and the security of information, which may be compromised.

Choice "2" is incorrect. Shared services is a consolidation of redundant services within an organization or group of affiliates. While consolidation of redundant services leads to efficiency, it may result in service flow disruption.

Choice "4" is incorrect. DMAIC is a methodology of Six Sigma that is applied to existing product and business process improvements. It stands for **D**efine the problem, **M**easure key aspects of the current process, **A**nalyze data, **I**mprove or optimize current processes, and **C**ontrol.

Topic D

QUESTION 1

Choice "1" is correct.

In this question, they want to know the operating income using a flexible budget. Certain actual and static budget data for the company is provided. The flexible budget will be for the actual 24,000 units.

The fixed costs for the flexible budget for the 24,000 units actually produced were the same as the static (master) budget for the 20,000 units, or $60,000. The variable costs will have to be converted to a per unit basis. Variable costs were 60% of sales ($120,000 / $200,000), or $6 per unit (the unit sales price of $10 × 0.60), with a contribution margin of 40% of sales or $4 per unit. At sales of 24,000 units, the contribution margin was $96,000 ($4 × 24,000). Subtracting the fixed costs produces a net income of $36,000 ($96,000 − $60,000).

Business V

QUESTION 2

Choice "4" is correct.

Sales forecasts are used as a basis for developing sales budgets. The sales budget drives the anticipated volume of production and needed capacity that is used for anticipating expenses.

Choice "1" is incorrect. Variance analysis is possible using a master budget. Although the results of variance analysis using a master budget may be distorted and therefore less useful as a result of differences in volume, variance analysis is not impossible using a master budget.

Choice "2" is incorrect. Master budgets are, indeed, generally and almost always developed on an annual basis, but the may be developed for different periods. The predominant characteristic of master budgets and other techniques is that it assumes one level of activity.

Choice "3" is incorrect. A flexible budget is not based on standards so much as it is based on different levels of activity. The flexible budget may act as a basis for developing standards, however, the flexible budget, in and of itself, does not create standards associated with required output for allowed output.

QUESTION 3

Choice "2" is correct.

In this question, they want to know which, if any, of a series of statements is/are correct. "All of the above" is an available option.

Statement I says that master budgets are normally confined to a single year for a single level of activity. Statement I is correct.

Statement II says that flexible budgets are financial plans prepared in a manner that allows for adjustments for changes in production or sales and accurately reflects expected costs for the adjusted output. Statement II is the definition of flexible budgets. Statement II is correct.

Statement III says that, normally, the first step in the preparation of Bronx's master budget for a year would be the preparation of its production budget. However, before the production budget can be prepared, a sales budget is needed. Statement III is incorrect.

Statement IV says that the success of Bronx's budgeting program will depend on the degree to which its top management accepts the program and how its management uses the budgeted data. Statement IV is correct.

QUESTION 4

Choice "3" is correct.

The problem requires the candidate to derive budgeted cash payments for the month of May from a series of assumptions provided by the budget. The components included in May's sales were assembled in April and purchased in March. Purchases were paid 75% in the month of purchase and 25% following the month of purchase. The cash budget for May would represent the 75% of the purchases in May and 25% of the purchases in April. May purchases relate to June assembly of July sales. April purchases relate to May assembly of June sales. ($8,000 × 75% + $7,000 × 25% = $7,750)

QUESTION 5

Choice "1" is correct.

In this question, they want to know the materials usage variance for a particular product. Certain data for the product is provided.

In this particular question, 8,400 pounds of material were used. 2,000 units of Brook were produced. The standard usage for 2,000 units was 8,000 pounds (2,000 × 4). The standard price was $2.50 per pound. Because the actual usage was greater than the standard usage, the materials usage variance must be unfavorable.

The variance formula for the materials usage variance can be stated as the standard price of $2.50 times the difference between the actual and standard usage of 400 pounds (8,400 − 8,000), or $1,000 (*unfavorable*).

QUESTION 6

Choice "4" is correct.

In this question, they want to know the labor rate variance for a particular product. Certain data for the product is provided.

In this question, 9,500 hours of labor were worked to produce the 2,500 units of the broadband router. The actual rate of the labor was thus $11 per hour ($104,500 / 9,500), slightly above the standard rate. Thus, any labor rate variance is going to have to be unfavorable.

The standard for the 9,500 hours worked to produce the 2,500 units was $95,000 (9,500 ×$10). The difference between the actual of $104,500 and the standard of $95,000 was $9,500.

Another way to work the same question is to use the formula. The variance formula for the labor rate variance can be stated as the actual hours worked times the difference between the actual and standard rates [9,500 × ($11 − $10)], or $9,500 (*unfavorable*).

QUESTION 7

Choice "2" is correct.

In this question, they want to know the variable overhead spending variance for a product. Certain data for the product are provided.

The actual hours used to produce the 4,000 units of Bedford were 8,200 hours, and the standard hours to produce 4,000 units were 8,000 hours. Variable overhead is based on labor hours. The actual variable overhead rate is $5.10 ($41,820 / 8,200).

The variance formula for the variable overhead spending variance can be stated as the actual hours of 8,200 hours times the difference between the actual and standard rates of $.10 ($5.10 − $5.00), or $820 (*unfavorable*).

Business V

QUESTION 8

MCQ-09128

Choice "3" is correct.

In this question, they want to know which of a series of statements is/are correct for a responsibility accounting system. "None of the above" is not an available option, and neither is "All of the above."

Statement I says that, in a cost SBU, managers are responsible for controlling costs but not revenue. Statement I is correct.

Statement II says that the idea behind responsibility accounting is that a manager should be held responsible for those items, and only those items, that the manager can actually control to a significant extent. Statement II is correct.

Statement III says that, to be effective, a good responsibility accounting system must provide for both planning and control. Planning without control and control without planning is not effective. Statement III is correct.

Statement IV says that common costs that are allocated to a SBU are normally controllable by the SBU's management. Common costs that are allocated are normally not controllable by an SBU's management. Statement IV is incorrect.

QUESTION 9

MCQ-09138

Choice "4" is correct.

In this question, they want to know which of a series of statements is/are correct.

Statement I says that a balanced scorecard reports management information regarding organizational performance in achieving goals classified by critical success factors to demonstrate that no single dimension of organizational performance can be relied upon to evaluate success. This statement is the definition of a balanced scorecard. Statement I is correct.

Statement II says that performance measures used in a balanced scorecard tend to be divided into financial, customer, internal business process, and learning and growth. Statement II is correct.

Statement III says that, in a balanced scorecard, internal business processes are what the company does in its attempts to satisfy customers. Statement III is correct.

Topic E

QUESTION 1

MCQ-09215

Choice "1" is correct.

The contribution margin from manufacturing (sales − variable costs) is $10 ($40 − $30) per unit sold, or $1,200,000 (120,000 units × $10). The fixed costs of manufacturing ($600,000) and selling and administrative costs ($400,000) are deducted from the contribution margin to arrive at an operating income of $200,000. The difference between the absorption income and the variable costing income is attributable to capitalization of the fixed manufacturing costs under the absorption method. Since 40% of the goods produced are still in inventory (80,000 / 200,000), 40% of the $600,000 in fixed costs, or $240,000, was capitalized under the absorption method. That amount was expensed under the variable costing method.

Business Final Review

QUESTION 2 — MCQ-09117

Choice "2" is correct.

The question requires computation of the breakeven point in dollars for a product. Certain cost and other data are provided.

Annual sales are $900,000, and the sales price is $20 per unit. That means 45,000 units were sold. $900,000 is one of the answers, but it cannot be the correct answer because there was a profit of $2 per unit and the question is asking for breakeven.

On a unit basis, total fixed overhead was $10 ($7 + $3). At 45,000 units, total fixed costs were $450,000.

To determine the breakeven point, it is necessary to determine the variable cost per unit. Prime cost (direct materials and direct labor) is given, and so are variable overhead and variable selling and administrative costs. Total variable costs are thus $8 ($6 + $1 + $1).

The breakeven equation for this question can be written as $20X = 8X + 450,000$, where X is the units sold at the breakeven point. Solving for X produces 37,500 units at $20 per unit, or $750,000 ($20 × 37,500).

Note: An alternative approach is to divide the total fixed costs by the contribution margin percentage. Fixed costs are $450,000. The contribution margin (sales minus variable costs) is $20 − $8 = $12. The contribution margin percentage is $12 / $20 = 60%. Fixed costs of $450,000 / 60% = $750,000.

QUESTION 3 — MCQ-09245

Choice "3" is correct.

Harbor would compare its variable costs of production and relevant (avoidable) fixed costs ($4.50). Costs are comprised of direct labor and direct material of $2.00 and the variable factory overhead of $1.00 along with avoidable fixed costs of $1.50 ($15,000/10,000) to arrive at total relevant costs of $4.50. Harbor would buy the bolts since its relevant production costs are greater than the proposed purchase price.

Choice "1" is incorrect. Harbor would need to consider more than its prime costs as part of the analysis.

Choice "2" is incorrect. Harbor would need to consider more than its variable costs as part of the analysis.

Choice "4" is incorrect. Harbor would not consider irrelevant fixed costs as part of the analysis.

QUESTION 4 — MCQ-09231

Choice "1" is correct.

Simple linear regression involves only one independent variable. Multiple linear regression analysis involve more than one independent variable.

Choice "2" is incorrect. Multiple linear regression analysis analyzes the impact of multiple independent variables (income, competitors, etc.) on a single dependent variable (revenue) not vice versa.

Choice "3" is incorrect. While non-linear multiple regression analysis may consider the dynamic relationships associated with multiple independent and dependent variables, multiple linear regression only considers the impact of multiple independent variables on a single dependent variable.

Choice "4" is incorrect. This is a distracter. Codependence has more to do with psychoanalysis than regression analysis.

Business V

MCQ-09168

Choice "4" is correct.

In this question, they want to know which statement is correct with respect to regression analysis. The only given fact is that there is a 0.90 correlation coefficient between the variables X and Y.

Statement I says that there is little relationship between X and Y. The correlation coefficient is the strength of the relationship between the independent and dependent variables X and Y. Because correlation coefficients range between −1.00 and 1.00, a correlation coefficient of 0.90 would indicate a strong relationship. Statement I is incorrect.

Statement II says that variation in X explains 90% of the variation in Y. This statement is discussing the coefficient of determination, not the correlation coefficient. Statement II is incorrect.

Statement III says that, if X increases, Y will never decrease. If the correlation were perfect with a correlation coefficient of 1.00, "never" would be correct. Statement III is incorrect.

Statement IV says that, if X increases, Y will generally increase. Statement IV is correct.

MCQ-09097

Choice "2" is correct.

In this question, they want to know the cost function from a set of data for units and costs using the high-low method.

The high level is the 1,900 units in February, and the low level is the 1,100 units in July. The costs for those months are $15,200 and $12,800. None of the other months are relevant because the high-low method uses only the high and low months.

The slope of the line is the change in cost of $2,400 ($15,200 − $12,800) divided by the change in activity of 800 (1,900 − 1,100), or $3 per unit.

The total cost of $15,200 less the variable cost of $5,700 for those units ($3 × 1,900), yields fixed cost of $9,500.